ヘルシング

HELLSING

ヘルシング

HELLSING

2

TWO

KOHTA HIRANO
平野耕太

translation
DUANE JOHNSON

lettering and retouch
WILBERT LACUNA
and **STUDIO CUTIE**

DARK HORSE MANGA

president and publisher
MIKE RICHARDSON
US editor
CHRIS WARNER
first edition editors
TIM ERVIN *and* **FRED LUI**
associate editor
JENNY BLENK
collection designer
SKYLER WEISSENFLUH
digital art technician
ADAM PRUETT

English-language version produced by DARK HORSE MANGA.

HELLSING vol. 2 by KOHTA HIRANO

Dark Horse Manga
A division of Dark Horse Comics LLC
10956 SE Main Street
Milwaukie OR 97222

DarkHorse.com

Represented in the EU by Authorised Rep Compliance Ltd.
Ground Floor, 71 Lower Baggot Street, Dublin, D02 P593, Ireland
ARCCompliance.com

To find a comics shop near you, visit FindYourComic.store.

Second edition: December 2023
ISBN 978-1-50673-851-2

5 7 9 10 8 6 4
Printed in the United States of America

Library of Congress Cataloging-in-Publication Data

Names: Hirano, Kohta, author. | Johnson, Duane, 1976- translator. | Lacuna, Wilbert, illustrator. | Studio Cutie, illustrator.
Title: Hellsing / Kohta Hirano ; translation, Duane Johnson ; lettering and retouch, Wilbert Lacuna and Studio Cutie.
Other titles: Herushingu. English
Description: Second edition. | Milwaukie OR : Dark Horse Manga, 2023-
Identifiers: LCCN 2023014695 (print) | LCCN 2023014696 (ebook) | ISBN 9781506738505 (v. 1 ; trade paperback) | ISBN 9781506738598 (v. 1 ; ebook)
Subjects: LCGFT: Comics (Graphic works) | Vampire comics. | Horror comics. | Graphic novels. | Manga.
Classification: LCC PN6790.J33 H5648613 2023 (print) | LCC PN6790.J33 (ebook) | DDC 741.5/952--dc23/eng/20230605
LC record available at https://lccn.loc.gov/2023014695
LC ebook record available at https://lccn.loc.gov/2023014696

HELLSING

ヘルシング

平野耕太

KOHTA HIRANO

CONTENTS

ORDER 07

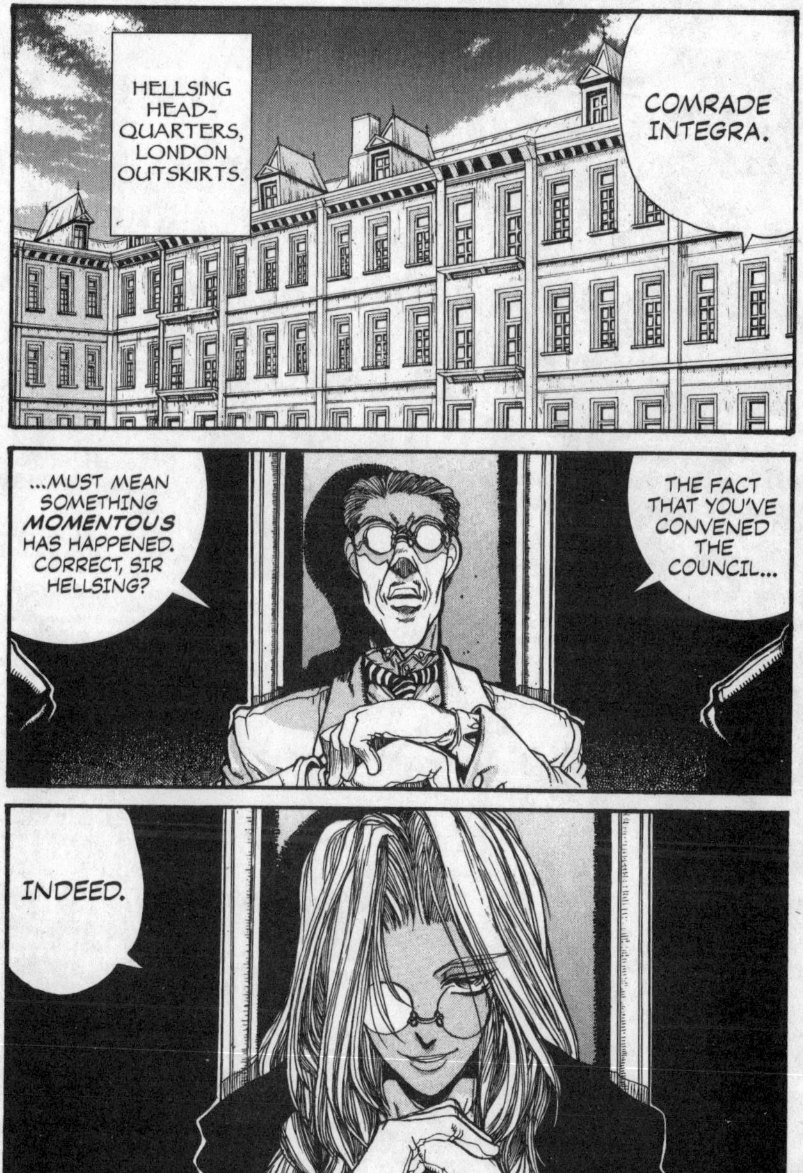
HELLSING HEAD-QUARTERS, LONDON OUTSKIRTS.
COMRADE INTEGRA.
THE FACT THAT YOU'VE CONVENED THE COUNCIL...
...MUST MEAN SOMETHING *MOMENTOUS* HAS HAPPENED. CORRECT, SIR HELLSING?
INDEED.

ORDER 07
デッドゾーン
DEAD ZONE 1

THE ROUND TABLE COUNCIL.
A SOCIETY MADE UP OF TWELVE INDIVIDUALS OF POLITICAL AND ECONOMIC PROMINENCE, NOBLES, AND MILITARY LEADERS, ALL LOYAL TO THE ENGLISH CROWN.
ESSENTIALLY, THIS IS THE SMALL GROUP THAT RUNS THE BRITISH EMPIRE FROM BEHIND THE SCENES.
THESE RECENT INCIDENTS...
THEY'RE TOO MUCH FOR US TO KEEP UNDER WRAPS.
WE CAN ONLY CONTROL SO MUCH INFORMATION.
HAVE YOU ASCERTAINED ANYTHING?
JA.
TNK
REGARDING ALL THE VAMPIRES AND GHOULS WE'VE VANQUISHED...
A THOROUGH INVESTIGATION WAS CONDUCTED.
WE NOW KNOW SOMETHING NEW.

AND WHAT WOULD *THAT* BE?
?!
THIS.
IT'S... SOMETHING LIKE A SPEECH CHIP.
THESE WERE EMBEDDED THROUGHOUT THE VAMPIRES' BODIES.
THEY DEFINE THE VAMPIRE'S STATUS, BEHAVIOUR, INTENT, AND AGGRESSION.
OR SO OUR INVESTIGATION SEEMS TO SUGGEST.
WHA--?!
GTUNK
タタッ
TNK
ガタ
WHAT THE *HELL?!*
THIS CHAIN OF VAMPYRIC INCIDENTS IS NO NATURAL OCCURRENCE.
OBVIOUSLY, SOMEONE'S *PULLING* THE *STRINGS.*

MURMUR MURMUR
MURMUR
MURMUR
MURMUR
AND ONE OTHER THING.
WH... WHAT, PRAY TELL?!
THERE'S *MORE?*
IT'S THE *GHOULS.*
ORIGINALLY GHOULS WERE THE RESULT OF VAMPIRE ATTACKS ON *NON-VIRGINS.*
BUT *NOT* THIS TIME!
OF ALL THE VICTIMS IN THE RECENT ATTACKS, NOT *ONE* OF THEM BECAME A VAMPIRE.
EVEN YOUNG BOYS AND GIRLS, *OBVIOUSLY* VIRGINS, ALL TURNED INTO *GHOULS!*
HISTORICALLY, GHOULS ARE DESTROYED WHEN THEIR MASTER VAMPIRE CEASES TO EXIST.
BUT IN THIS LAST INCIDENT IN BADRICK, THE VATICAN'S FATHER ANDERSON HAD ALREADY KILLED THE VAMPIRE...
AND THE PLACE WAS *SWARMING* WITH GHOULS WHEN WE SENT IN OUR MEN.

MEANWHILE, THIRTY METERS BELOW.
THE BASEMENT.
W... WALTER...
WHAT... EXACTLY... *IS* THAT?
WELL...
THAT WOULD BE A *COFFIN.*
GONNNNG
RIGHT, THEN *WHY?*
WHY'S SUCH A THING IN MY ROOM?
IT IS AT SIR INTEGRA'S COMMAND.
"I SUPPOSE VAMPIRES MUST SLEEP IN COFFINS."
TO QUOTE DIRECTLY, THAT IS.
CHATTA CHATTA SHIVER SHIVER
OOOOOOOO
DODODODODODODODODODO
...WHAT ABOUT MY *BED...?*
RIGHT, I *DISPOSED* OF THAT.
KCHING
ARGGGH!
SHOOO
BGOGOGOGOGOGOGOGO
SHMP
NOOOOOOO!
ZUBAAAN
CHKING
BGOGOGOGOGOGOGOGO

NGWALLLLL-DERRRRRR!
GRRRRRRRRRRR!
BGOGOGOGOGO
COME NOW... THAT'S NOT ALL.
THE HONORABLE ALUCARD HAS AN ORDER FOR YOU AS WELL.
MASTER?
THE SAME.
SINCE BECOMING A VAMPIRE...
YOU HAVE YET TO DRINK ANY BLOOD.
!!
SO YOU MUST AT LEAST SLEEP IN A COFFIN IN THE SOIL WHERE YOU WERE BORN.
OTHERWISE, YOUR POWERS WILL WEAKEN.
....
WHY DO YOU REFUSE TO DRINK?
IS IT SUCH AN EVIL THING TO PARTAKE OF DONATED BLOOD?

I DON'T KNOW...
BUT... IF I DO DRINK THE BLOOD,
IT FEELS LIKE SOMETHING WILL HAVE ENDED FOREVER...
....
....
DEAR ME,
WHAT A BOTHER.
WHAT A PISSANT.
OOOOPS
!
MASTER!!
I'M STARTING TO WISH I'D NEVER BOTHERED TO SUCK YOUR BLOOD.
YOU COULD'VE DIED AS A HUMAN THEN, HAD YOU CHOSEN TO.

BUT YOU CHOSE THE *NIGHT.*
NO MATTER HOW MUCH YOU LONG FOR THE LIGHT OF DAY...
...ALL IT WOULD DO IS EAT AWAY AT YOUR BODY.
LISTEN TO *ME*, POLICE GIRL.
ONCE YOU DENY THE MORNING SUN AND BEGIN TO WALK THE NIGHT, YOU CAN NEVER, *EVER* TURN BACK TO THE DAY!
....
...!
HNNNN
BUT MAYBE THIS TOO COULD WORK.
THERE MAY BE A PLACE FOR A TIMID *"EVENING WALKER"* LIKE YOU.
R--
RIGHT!

ON THAT NOTE, I FINISHED WHAT WE WERE DISCUSSING, ALUCARD.
O-HO!
SHOW IT TO ME.
I WAS JUST ABOUT TO, ACTUALLY...
ゴトッ
TUNK
ガパッ
GPOK
!
HAHA... WELL, WELL...
THE 13mm ANTI-FREAK COMBAT PISTOL **JACKAL.**
UNLIKE THE .454 CASULL YOU'VE **BEEN** USING, IT USES A NEW TYPE OF CUSTOM ROUNDS.
Jesus Christ is in Heaven now
39cm LONG, 16kg, SIX ROUND MAGAZINE.
THIS ISN'T SOMETHING A **HUMAN** COULD HANDLE.

CUSTOMIZED 13mm ARMOR-PIERCING EXPLOSIVE ROUNDS.
チャキッ
KCHIK
THE CASINGS?
MADE FROM PURE *MACEDONIUM* SILVER.
GUNPOWDER?
MARVELLS CHEMICALS CARTRIDGE *N.N.A.9.*
AND THE TIPS? EXPLOSIVE? MERCURY?
MERCURY TIPS, BLESSED IN ADVANCE.
IT'S *PERFECT,* WALTER.
MY *UTMOST* THANKS.

WITH THIS, I BET I COULD EVEN TAKE DOWN ANDERSON.
FWPP
IS THAT SO?
IT'S THAT POWERFUL?
WE TOOK THE LIBERTY OF REDESIGNING YOUR WEAPON TOO, MISS POLICE GIRL.
ha ha ha!
HUH?!
HRNN!
KCHAK
HNN!

KLAK
THE 30mm ANTI-MIDIAN CANNON, HARKONNEN.
CHATTA CHATTA SHIVER SHIVER
CHATTA CHATTA CHATTA
THERE ARE TWO TYPES OF AMMO, DEPLETED URANIUM SHELLS AND ARMOR-PIERCING INCENDIARY ROUNDS!!
IT CAN FUNCTION AS AN ANTI-TANK RIFLE, ELIMINATING ALL TARGETS BOTH ON LAND AND IN THE AIR.
WHA...
WHA...
WHA?!
GYAHHHH
WHA--?
WHA--?
...WHAT THE BLOODY HELL?!

REAR GATE
SHF SHF
ザッザッ
SHF SHF
ザッザッ
SO 'COURSE HE **LOST IT** AND **FREAKED OUT**.
ANNOYIN' PRICK.
HEY, YOU AGREE WITH ME, RIGHT BRO?
YOU **ALWAYS** TALK TOO MUCH BEFORE WE DO A JOB.
JUST BE **COOL** AND DO YOUR THING.
YEAH YEAH YEAH, THAT SHIT AGAIN.
I HEAR YOU, **LOUD** AND **CLEAR**.
WE HAVEN'T HAD A GIG THIS **BIG** IN SOME TIME.
FAILURE'S **NOT** AN OPTION.

FAILURE? NOT A *FUCKIN'* CHANCE.
THIS IS GONNA BE A *CAKEWALK!*

FWEEEET
LOOK HERE, YOU TWO!
THIS IS A RESTRICTED AREA!!
BEEP
AHH, I'M SO SORRY.
ピッ
WE'RE PART OF A SIGHT-SEEING TOUR, SIR.
WE'RE TOURING THE UK'S OLD ARISTOCRATIC MANSIONS AND CASTLES.
THIS PLACE ISN'T OPEN TO THE PUBLIC?
THIS IS PRIVATE PROPERTY.
YOU MUST LEAVE AT ONCE!
POLICE

THMP
ドス
POLIC
POLICE
SNAP
SSSSSSS
?!!
SHLLUP
KCHAK
KCHAK
KCHAK

....
...?!
YOU LOOK PALE.
SURE YOU'RE ALRIGHT?
SNAP!
Ciao!
DM DM DM DM DM DM DM DM
DM DM DM DM DM DM DM DM DM DM DM

BRRRRRAP
CEASE FIRE!!
STOP!
BRRRRRAP
BRP
BRRAP
GOD-DAMMIT STOP!
PAP PAP
BRRAP
BRO, THESE GUYS ARE A BUNCHA DUMBASS RETARDS. YOU SURE 'BOUT THEM?
HM...
SSSSSSSSSSSSSS
THEY'RE AN EXPERIMENT. JUST A BUNCH OF WORTHLESS CANNON FODDER.
TO HIM, WE'RE ALL PROBABLY NOTHING MORE THAN COGS IN THE MACHINE.

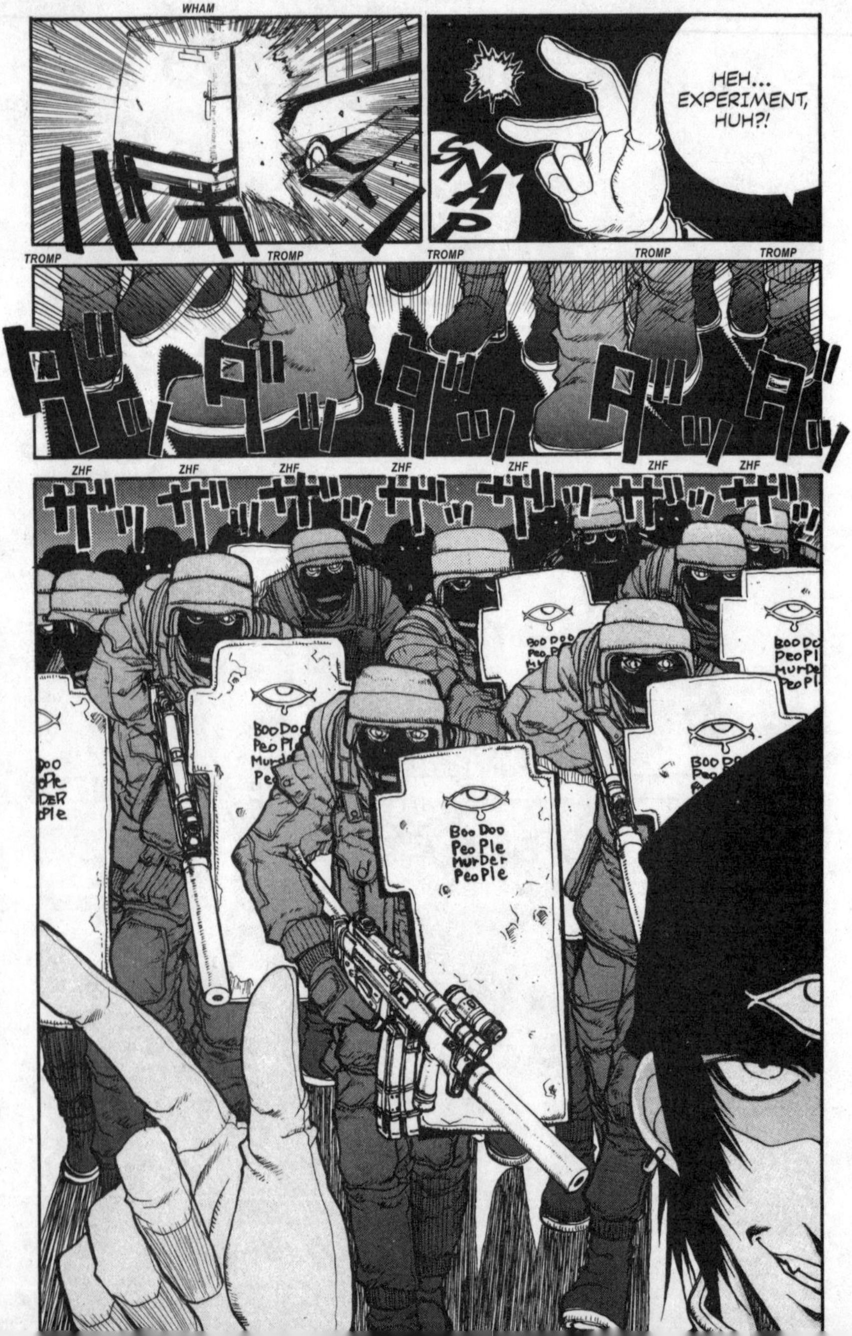
WHAM
SNAP
HEH... EXPERIMENT, HUH?!
TROMP
TROMP
TROMP
TROMP
TROMP
ZHF
ZHF
ZHF
ZHF
ZHF
ZHF
ZHF
Boo Doo People Murder People

CHAK
WORKS FOR ME, MAN. SO IT'S ALL WORTHLESS AS SHIT!
AS LONG AS WE GET TA MAKE THE KILL AND DRINK THE SPILL...
...WHO GIVES A FUCK?
HELLSING? WHATEVER, MAN.
CHCHAK
CHCHAK
ALUCARD? WHAT THE FUCK EVER, MAN!
WE!
...ARE GONNA WIPE ALL YOU BITCHES OUT!

!
EH!
WHAT IS IT?!
WHAT'S GOING ON, INTEGRA?!
THIS IS THE MAIN GUARD POST, SIR INTEGRA!!
WHAT? WHAT'S HAPPENING?
THE ENEMY! WE'RE UNDER ATTACK!
EXCUSE ME?!
WE CAN'T MAKE CONTACT WITH THE OUTSIDE! WE'RE CURRENTLY ENGAGED AT THE MAIN GROUND FLOOR ENTRYWAY!!
HOLD THEM OFF! BUY US SOME TIME!!
UH, BUT! BUT....! THE ENEMY...!
CALM DOWN! HOW MANY ARE THERE?!
GIVE ME SOME DETAILS!
BLAM
THEY'RE...
THEY'RE GHOULS!!

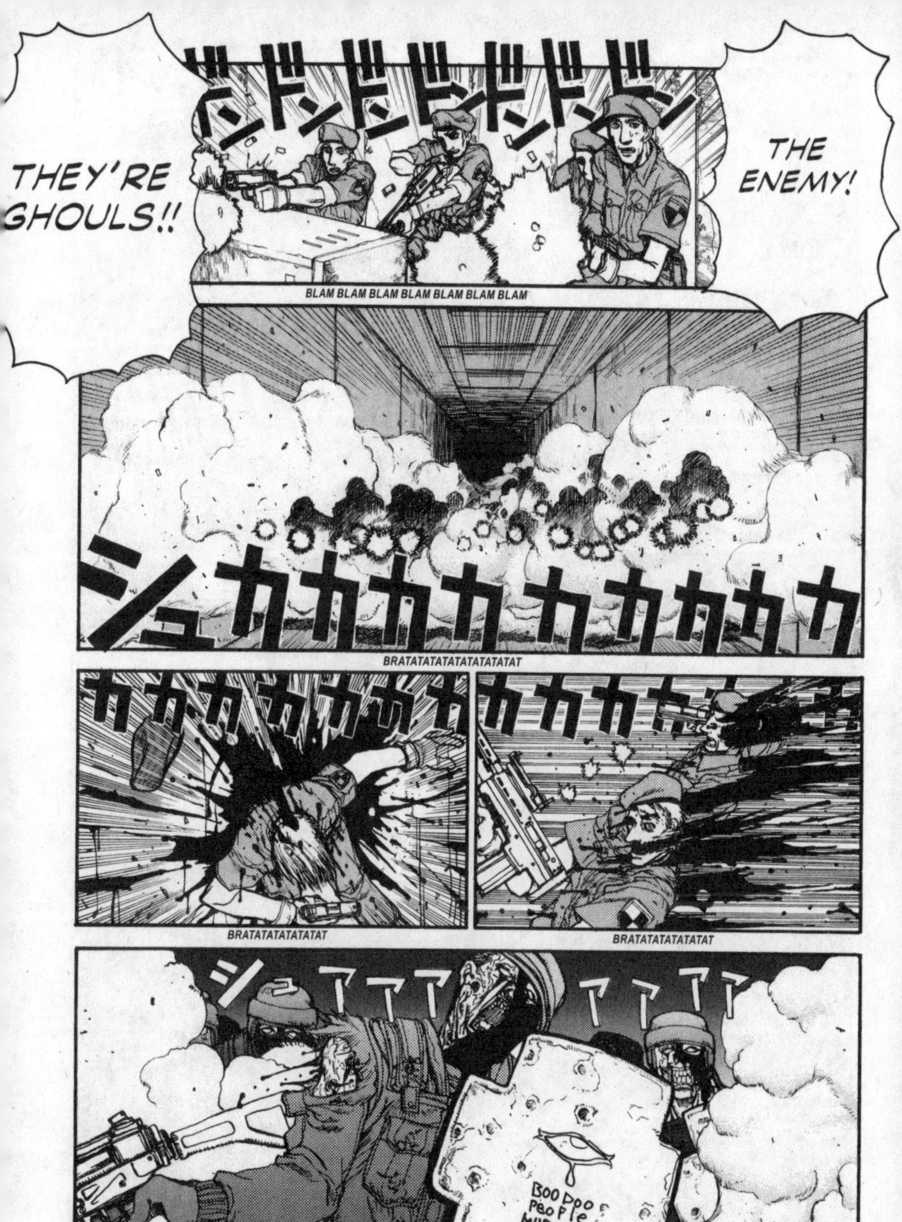
THE ENEMY!
THEY'RE GHOULS!!
BLAM BLAM BLAM BLAM BLAM BLAM BLAM
BRATATATATATATATATATAT
BRATATATATATATAT
BRATATATATATATAT
BOO DOO PEOPLE MURDER PEOPLE
SHHHAAAAA

ZHF ザッ
ZHF ザッ
ZHF ザッ
ZHF ザッ
ZHF ザッ
ZHF ザッ
ZHF ザッ
ZHF ザッ
NYAAHAHAHAHA
HAHAHAHAHAHA!
DAMN THIS GIVES ME SUCH A WOODY!!
WE GET A GOD MODE CHEAT AND YOU DON'T!!

AN ARMY...
...OF GHOULS?!
LOOK, JUST BUY US SOME TIME!!
ざわざわざわ
MURMUR MURMUR
EVACUATING THE COUNCIL MEMBERS IS OUR TOP PRIORITY.
WHAT ABOUT THE ROOFTOP HELICOPTER...?
ドガッ
BADOOM
!!
WHAT WAS THAT...?!
I THINK THAT WAS THE HELICOPTER BEING DESTROYED!
WE'RE FINISHED! THE ENEMY IS ALMOST...

*: PRONOUNCED (YON)

ARE YA READY TA HUNKER DOWN IN A CORNER AND BEG FOR MERCY?
HAVE YA PISSED YER PANTS? HAVE YA PRAYED TA GOD?
WE'RE GONNA COME ICE YOU NOW.
HEY, YOU MAY EVEN STILL HAVE TIME TO GO FOR OUR SPECIAL SUICIDE OFFER.
HIGHLY RECOMMENDED!
SEE YA AROUND! I LOVE YOU ALL, PIGS!
SOOEE!
KSH-- KSHHH!
WHAT IN BLOODY HELL IS THIS, INTEGRA?!
WE'RE UNDER ATTACK.
INTELLIGENCE APPEARS TO HAVE BEEN LEAKED.
YOU DON'T SEEM TOO CON-CERNED...!
WALTER. WALTER, WHERE ARE YOU?
YOU SAID... WE'RE BEING ATTACKED?!
YES, MY LADY!

IN MISS SERAS' ROOM, DOWNSTAIRS.
I AM AWARE OF THE SITUATION.
IT WILL BE ABOUT FOUR TO FIVE HOURS BEFORE THE MILITARY POLICE NOTICE THIS MESS AND DEPLOY.
UNTIL THEN, WE MUST DIG OUR HEELS IN AND PROTECT THE COUNCIL ROOM.
BTUMP TUMP TUMP TUMP
WHAT DO YOU ADVISE?
VWIP
AS I HAVE ALUCARD AND MISS SERAS HERE...
WE WILL DIVIDE INTO TWO GROUPS, ONE OF WHICH WILL COME TO YOUR DEFENSE.
AND THE OTHER WILL BE THE OFFENSE. HOW DOES THIS SOUND?
SHHP
THINK BACK TO TEN YEARS AGO.
HOW DID YOU REACH ALUCARD UNDER-GROUND?
THERE IS ONLY ONE WAY IN OR OUT.
IN SHORT, PROTECT THE ONE DOORWAY AT ALL COSTS.
HOW WILL YOU GET HERE?!
THE PATH IS LITTERED WITH GHOULS!
VENTILA-TION SHAFTS?!
CORRECT.
JUST WAIT, WE'LL BE THERE SHORTLY.

WALTER, THEY...
THE BASTARDS ATE MY MEN.
KLICK
...THEY WILL NOT GET AWAY WITH THIS.
DO NOT LET THEM LEAVE THIS PLACE ALIVE.
ヒュパッ
BUT OF COURSE, MY DEAR SIR INTEGRA.
カッ
KAKK

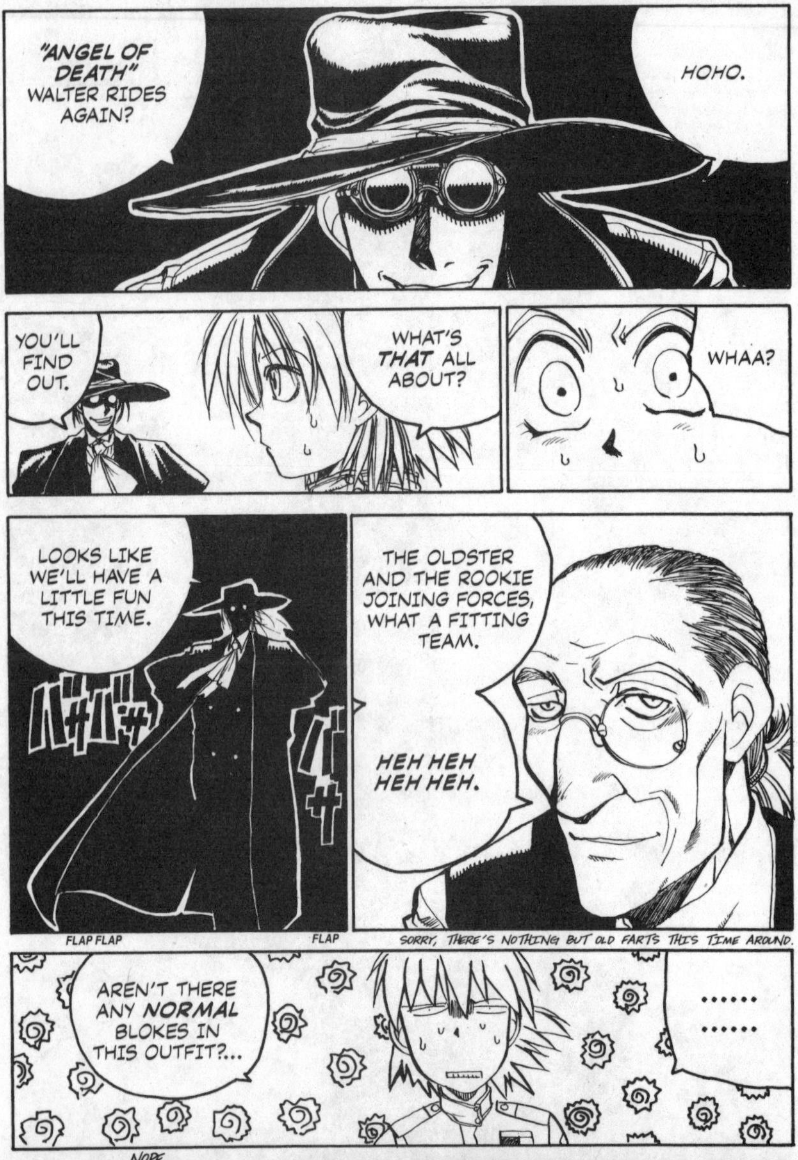
HOHO.
"ANGEL OF DEATH" WALTER RIDES AGAIN?
WHAA?
WHAT'S THAT ALL ABOUT?
YOU'LL FIND OUT.
THE OLDSTER AND THE ROOKIE JOINING FORCES, WHAT A FITTING TEAM.
HEH HEH HEH HEH.
SORRY, THERE'S NOTHING BUT OLD FARTS THIS TIME AROUND.
LOOKS LIKE WE'LL HAVE A LITTLE FUN THIS TIME.
FLAP
FLAP FLAP
......
......
AREN'T THERE ANY NORMAL BLOKES IN THIS OUTFIT?...
NOPE.

ORDER 07 / END

HELLO HELLO, WASSUP, BRO? CAN YOU HEAR ME?
THIS IS JAN, CONQUEROR OF THE HELLSING ARMY! OHHHHH YEAHHH!
DOMINATION OF THE FIRST AND SECOND FLOORS HERE IS ABOUT COMPLETE!
NOW WE JUST GOTTA BUST INTO THE ALMIGHTY COUNCIL...
...AND BEAT DOWN THE DUMBASS BROAD AND THE GERIATRIC BUNCH!
PROCEED AS PLANNED, THEN. DO NOT LET ME DOWN.
I'M ABOUT TO MOVE TOWARDS THE BASEMENT.
NOW, TIME TO SEE JUST HOW YOUR SPECS RATE.
VAMPIRE ALUCARD.

ORDER 08

DEAD ZONE②

デッド ゾーン

WHAT IN GOD'S NAME IS *GOING ON* HERE?!
EXPLAIN, INTEGRA!!
THE ENEMY IS COMING, AND SOON.
THE FIRST TWO FLOORS HAVE FALLEN, WE HAVE NOWHERE LEFT TO RUN.
THAT *ISN'T* WHAT I'M *ASKING!!*
WHO IS GOING TO TAKE RESPONSI-BILITY FOR--
THIS IS NOT THE *TIME* FOR SUCH THINGS, SIR PENWOOD.
WHAT'S IMPORTANT IS, IF THE TIME COMES, *HOW WE ARE TO PROTECT OURSELVES?*
ISN'T THAT RIGHT, INTEGRA?
AYE.
B...BUT AREN'T THESE THINGS UNDEAD GHOULS?!
THIS IS PREPOSTEROUS...!!

CLANG CLANG CLUNK

WHOK

HN!
HUH?
HN-NNNN-NNNNNNN!
WHAT THE? HNNNNN!
KREEEE
ギギギ
WHOA!
FWOP
ガコーーッ
OWWWWW...
ステーン
WHUMP
ARE YOU ALRIGHT, MISS SERAS?
スタ
TAKK
WALTER!
LIKEWISE, I'M SORRY *I'M* LATE...
カッカッ
KATZ KATZ

HOW WAS THE SITUATION DOWN-STAIRS?
OUR DEFENSES HAVE ALMOST BEEN ANNIHILATED.
TRULY, IT RESEMBLES A SCENE FROM **HELL**.
WE NEVER ANTICIPATED THE TACTIC OF ARMING A LARGE GROUP OF GHOULS...
...AND USING THEM FOR A SYSTEMATIC ADVANCE. I DON'T KNOW WHOM, BUT SOMEONE PLANNED THIS QUITE WELL.
WALTER, I'LL BE FRANK.
IS THIS THE END FOR ALL OF US?
NO!!
NOT IN THE ***LEAST!!***
ヒッ
VWIP

COMPARED TO WHAT THE FIRST SIR HELLSING HAD TO DEAL WITH A CENTURY AGO...
...THIS IS HARDLY WHAT I WOULD CALL A PINCH.
IT WILL BE AN AMBUSH, ALUCARD FROM THE BASEMENT, AND US FROM THE THIRD FLOOR.
AS YOU ORDERED, MY LADY.
NO, MAKE THAT A ***SORTIE***.
WE WON'T LET ONE OF THE VERMIN ESCAPE FROM THIS PLACE.
LET US ***TEACH*** THAT ***BRAT*** JUST HOW EXPENSIVE THE ***TUITION***...
...FOR A ***HELLSING*** EDUCATION CAN BE.

AH SHIT, THIS PISSES ME OFF! IT REALLY FUCKIN' PISSES ME OFF!
REALLY!
THERE'S JUST TOO BIG A CLASS DIVISION IN ENGLAND...
AN' THIS BOURGEOIS BITCH IS SMOKIN' OVERPRICED CIGARS!
KATZ KATZ KATZ KATZ KATZ
CRAP!
KATZ KATZ KATZ KATZ
I'M NOT GONNA LET THAT BITCH DIE EASY.
WHAM

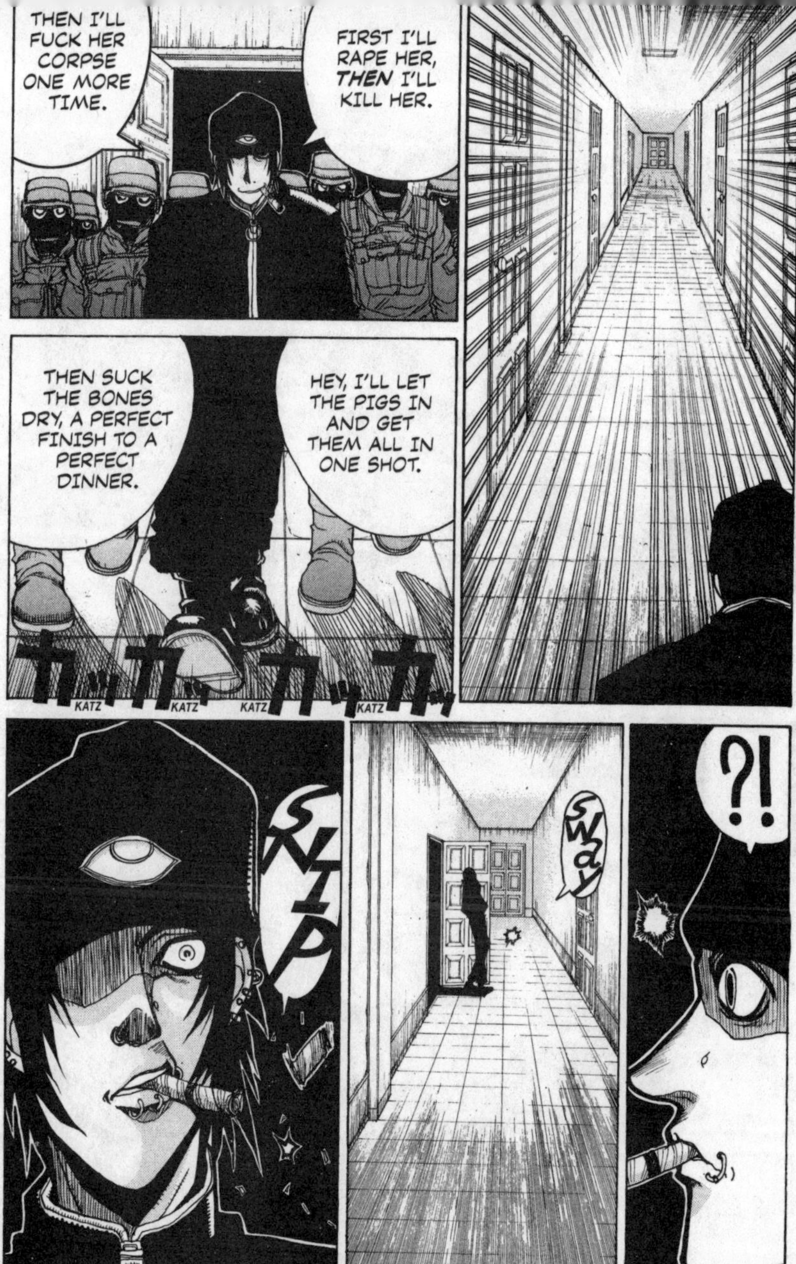
FIRST I'LL RAPE HER, THEN I'LL KILL HER.
THEN I'LL FUCK HER CORPSE ONE MORE TIME.
HEY, I'LL LET THE PIGS IN AND GET THEM ALL IN ONE SHOT.
THEN SUCK THE BONES DRY, A PERFECT FINISH TO A PERFECT DINNER.
KATZ
KATZ
KATZ
KATZ
?!
SWAY
SNIP

SPLUTT
PLIP
KATZ KATZ
KATZ KATZ
I MISSED...
I GUESS I'M NOT AS SHARP AS I USED TO BE.
!?!
...!
WHA--?!

WALTER C. DORNEZ, HELLSING FAMILY BUTLER.
FORMER *TRASHMAN* FOR THE ORDER OF ROYAL PROTESTANT KNIGHTS.
HERE I COME.
WHIPP

SH--!
....
SHOOT 'EM!!
SNAP
KCHAK KCHAK KCHAK KCHAK KCHAK
FWSSSH
BRATATATATATATAT

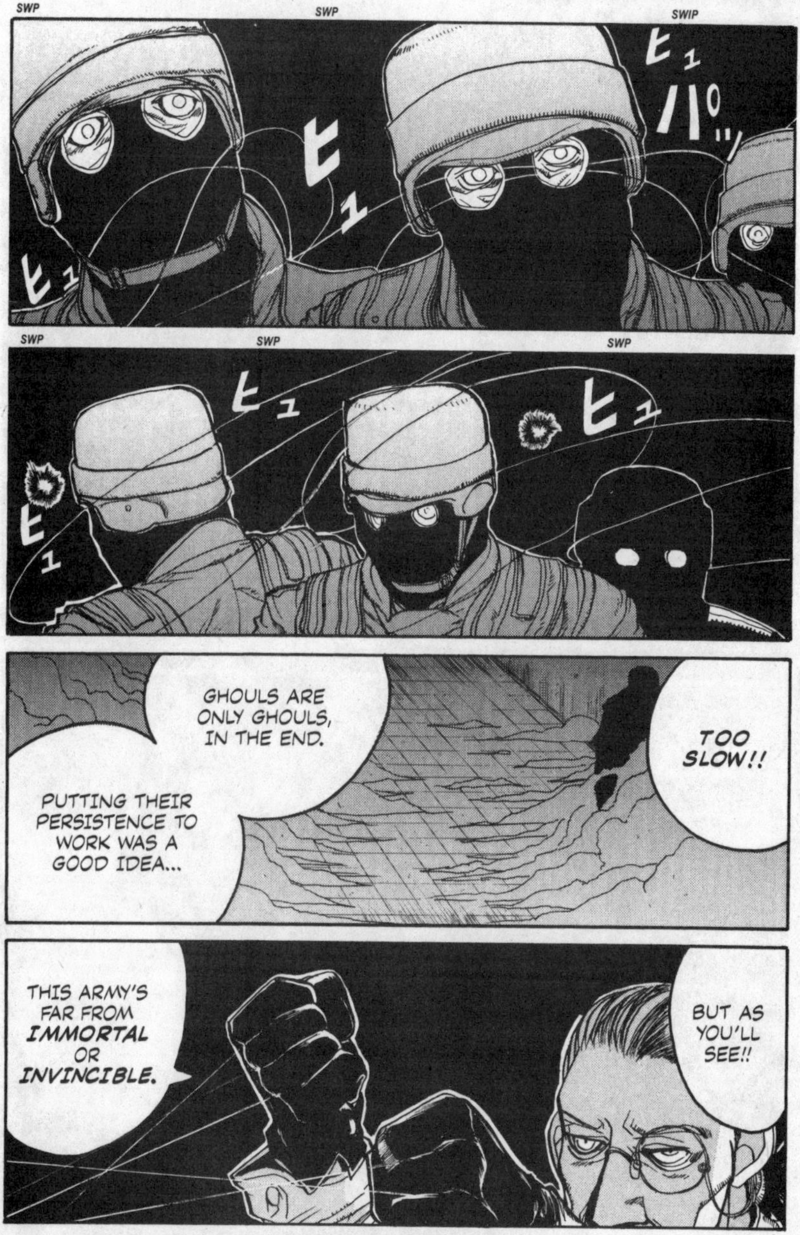
SWP
SWP
SWIP
SWP
SWP
SWP
GHOULS ARE ONLY GHOULS, IN THE END.
PUTTING THEIR PERSISTENCE TO WORK WAS A GOOD IDEA...
TOO SLOW!!
THIS ARMY'S FAR FROM IMMORTAL OR INVINCIBLE.
BUT AS YOU'LL SEE!!

SHLLLLORP
ARE YOU READY TO HUNKER DOWN IN A CORNER AND BEG FOR MERCY?
HAVE YOU PISSED YOUR PANTS?
PRAYED TO GOD?

FWEHEHA... HAHAH HAHEEHEEHEEHA HAHHH HAHH HAHAHAH!
RIGHT, RIGHT! THIS'S HOW IT SHOULD BE!
I WAS JUST STARTIN' TA THINK THIS WAS TOO FUCKIN' EASY, GRAMPS!
SNAP
Boo Doo Pea Ple MUR DER Peo Ple
Boo Doo Peo Ple MUR DER Peo Ple
SHNKK
KCHAK
KCHAK
KCHAK
KCHAK
!!
OH...MY.

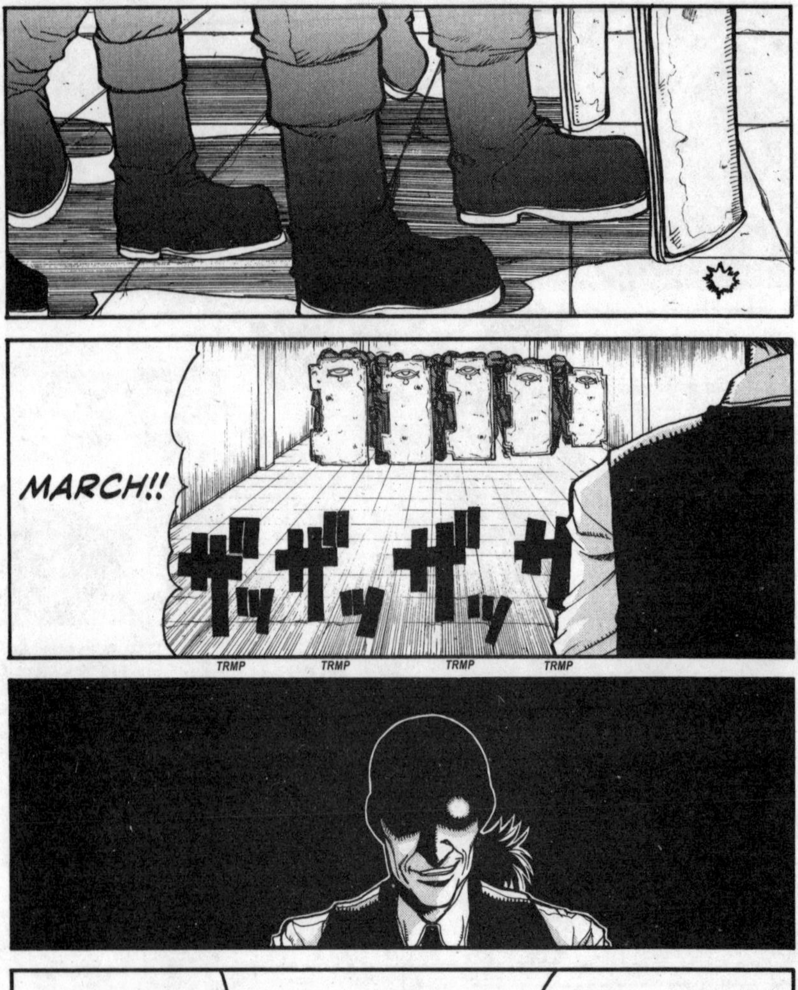
MARCH!!
TRMP
TRMP
TRMP
TRMP
MISS SERAS...
COMMENCE DIRECT FIRE SUPPORT!

Y...YEAH!
BASOOOM

BWOCK
SPAKOW
?!
WH...
WHOA...!
SECOND VOLLEY! RIGHT DOWN THE CENTER OF THE ENEMY LINE! INCENDIARY HIGH-EXPLOSIVE ROUNDS WITH VT FUSE! FORMULA #4, THE RED ONE!

★ SEEKING AN ASSISTANT!! SOMEONE WELL MOTIVATED, AROUND 20 OR SO. I'M ABOUT TO DIE AT THIS RATE. SOMEONE WHO CAN COMMUTE TO ADACHI WARD IN TOKYO. WOULD BE NEEDED 7-10 DAYS A MONTH. PLEASE SEND YOUR PORTFOLIO, ETC., TO OUR EDITORIAL OFFICE. YOUR RESUME AS WELL. THANK YOU AND GOOD LUCK.

BDOOM
I DREW IT TOO BIG. SORRY
BAKOOOM
CHCHAK
HEE! HEEHAH!
HEEHAA HAA HAHA!
VMMM

!
ZZTACK
SHHHAAH!
WHOM
ドカ
HYAAHAA
PATA
PATA
PATA
バラバラバラ
TCH!
Hellsing

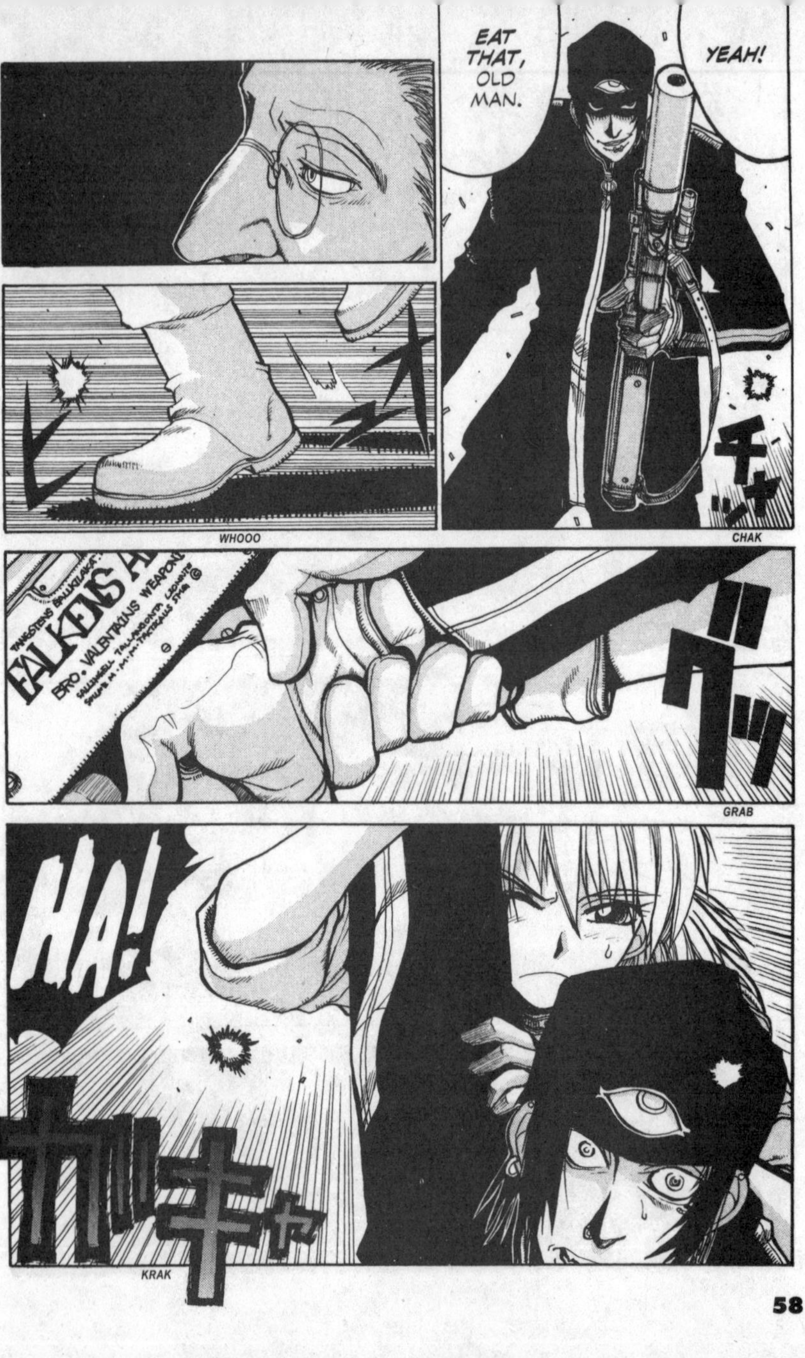
EAT THAT, OLD MAN.
YEAH!
CHAK
WHOOO
GRAB
HA!
KRAK

WALTER, ARE YOU OKAY?!
W--!
ギリギリギリ
ギリギリ
ARGHHHHHH!
GNNNN!
GNNN!
WHA... WHAT THE HELL WAS THAT!?!
AH-OW! OW OW OW OWWWW!
ARE YOU ALL RIGHT?
DEAR ME, I HAVEN'T GOT IT THE WAY I USED TO!
HNNNNN!
BUT WHEREVER DID YOU LEARN THAT TECHNIQUE?
WELL, YOU KNOW, I *WAS* A POLICE GIRL...
OW OW OW
NNN!
NNN! GNN!
!!
HEY, YOU! *BITCH!!*

YER A VAMPIRE, AIN'T YA?!
NOBODY TOLD ME HELLSING HAD SOMEBODY LIKE YOU HERE!
WHO THE HELL ARE YOU?!
S...STUPID LITTLE...
WHAT'S YOUR OBJECTIVE? YOU COULDN'T HAVE PUT THIS ARMY TOGETHER ALONE.
IS SOMEONE PULLING YOUR STRINGS?
GRAHHH! OW! OW! OW! OW! HNNNN!
I'LL TELL YA IF YA KISS MY ASS.
SENILE OLD GEEZER!!
GYEE!
ボキッ
KRAKK
I'LL ASK ONCE MORE, YOUNG MAN.
NEXT WE'LL TRY YOUR LEFT HAND.

...HEH!
WE WAS ONLY TOLD TWO THINGS!
"BUST UP THE SECRET BRITISH ORGANIZATION ORDER OF ROYAL PROTESTANT KNIGHTS AND THE ROUND TABLE COUNCIL!
"THEN COMPLETELY WIPE OUT THE ***VAMPIRE ALUCARD!!***"
"WE"? DID I HEAR YOU SAY ***"WE"?***
HUHYE HEHEH HEHAHAA!
RIGHT ABOUT NOW, MY BIG BROTHER'S...
...KICKIN' THE UNDEAD ***SHIT*** OUTTA ALUCARD.
ORDER 08 / END

Cola
Jan Valentine

GEHA HAA HAH HAHA HAH!
HNNNN!
~~~~!
HAHA HAAA!
WE GOT TWO OBJECTIVES!! PULVERIZIN' THE CONVENTION OF TWELVE...
!!
...AND WIPIN' OUT THAT VAMPIRE ALUCARD!!
WHA--!
WHAT?!
HYE HEH HA HAAA!
RIGHT ABOUT NOW, MY BIG BROTHER'S...
...ERASIN' ALUCARD FROM ANY AN' ALL EXISTENCE.
~~~~

ORDER 09
デッドゾーン
DEAD ZONE③
HELLSING
HELLSING
ENGLAND with the WORLD
HARKONNEN 30mm
ANTI MIDIAN CANNON
D. U. Shell
HELLSING
we will never give up and despair
we are on a mission from
GOD

BADASSSH
バラバラバラ
PATA
PATA
PATA

YOU'RE THERE, **AREN'T** YOU? COME ON **OUT**!
VAMPIRE ALUCARD.
EVEN IF YOU HIDE, I CAN SENSE YOUR POWERFUL ***CHI*** RISING UP FROM THIS PLACE.
I KNOW YOU'RE DOWN THERE.
カッ KATZ
カッ KATZ
カッ KATZ
WHERE **ARE** YOU?
!!

"EVEN IF I HIDE?"
I'M NOT RUNNING OR HIDING.
I JUST GOT A BIT TIRED OF WAITING FOR YOU.

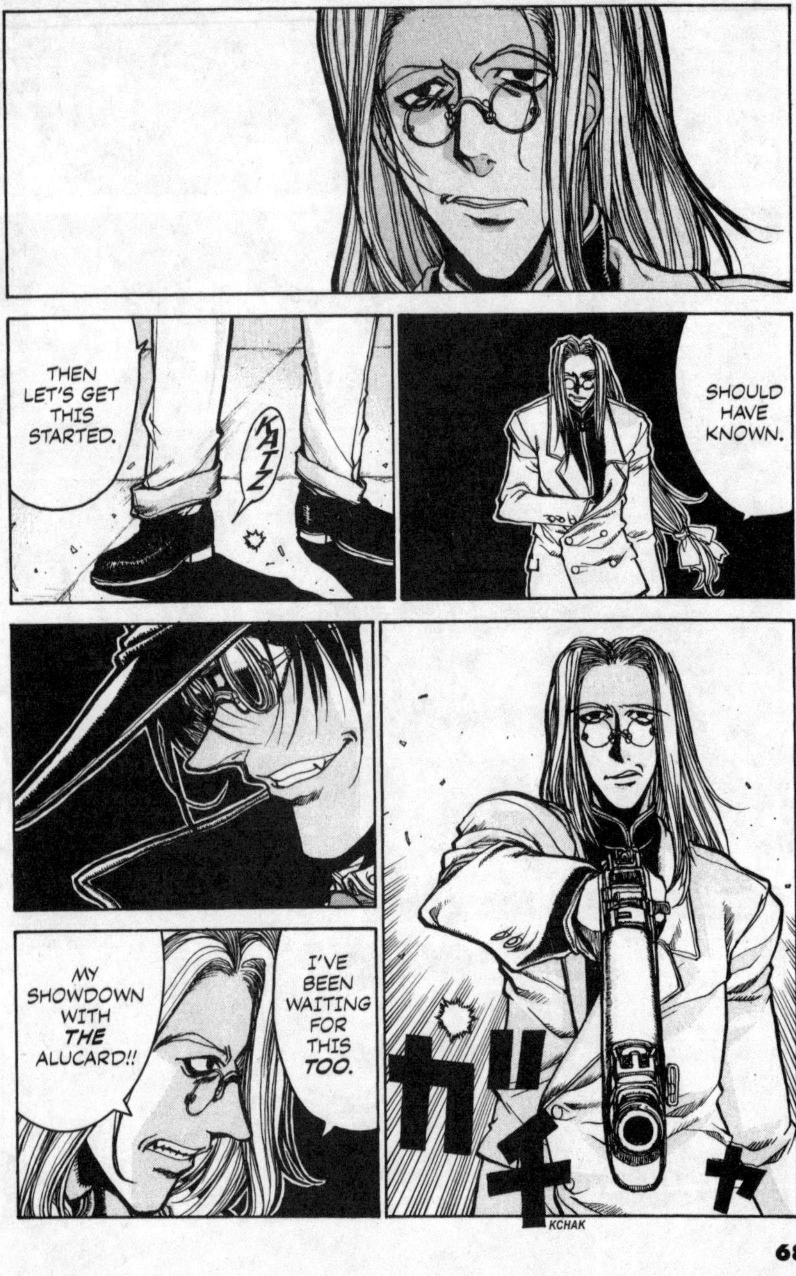
SHOULD HAVE KNOWN.
THEN LET'S GET THIS STARTED.
KATZ
ガチャ
KCHAK
I'VE BEEN WAITING FOR THIS *TOO.*
MY SHOWDOWN WITH ***THE*** ALUCARD!!

TIME TO CHECK OUT...
WSHAHH
WSHAHH
SHAA
SHP
SHP
SHP
SHP
SHP
SHP

WHPPP
YOU'RE QUICK.
BETTER NOT THINK I'M JUST ANOTHER ONE OF THOSE INSTANTS.
I'LL REPLACE YOU AS THE NEW NUMBER ONE!

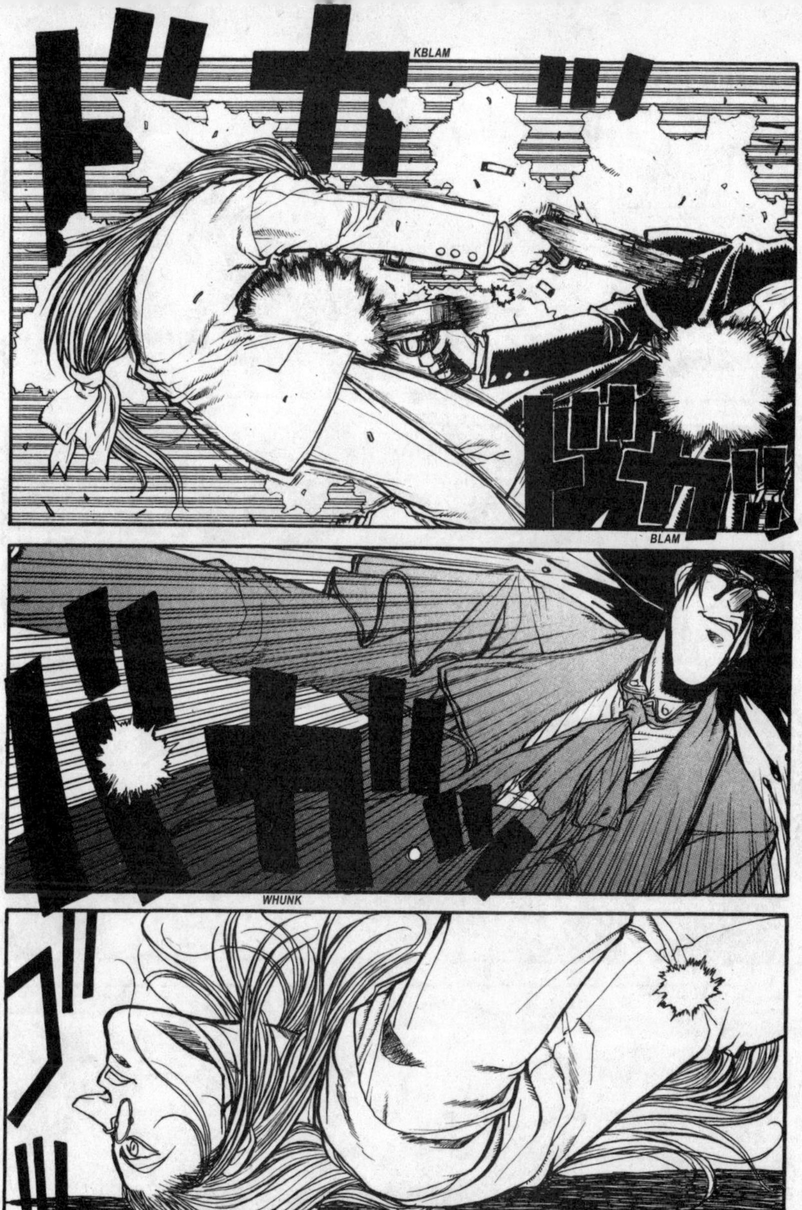
KBLAM
BLAM
WHUNK
WHUDD

OHHHHHHHHN
HEH... HE HAH...!
EHA HAHA! HAHA HA!
HEH HEH HEH HEHEH!
HEHEH... HEHE HEH.
HEHE HEH! HEHE HEH!
LIFT

CH-CHACK
ドカドカドカ
BLAM
BLAM
BLAM
LUNGE

CHOK
WHPP
POW

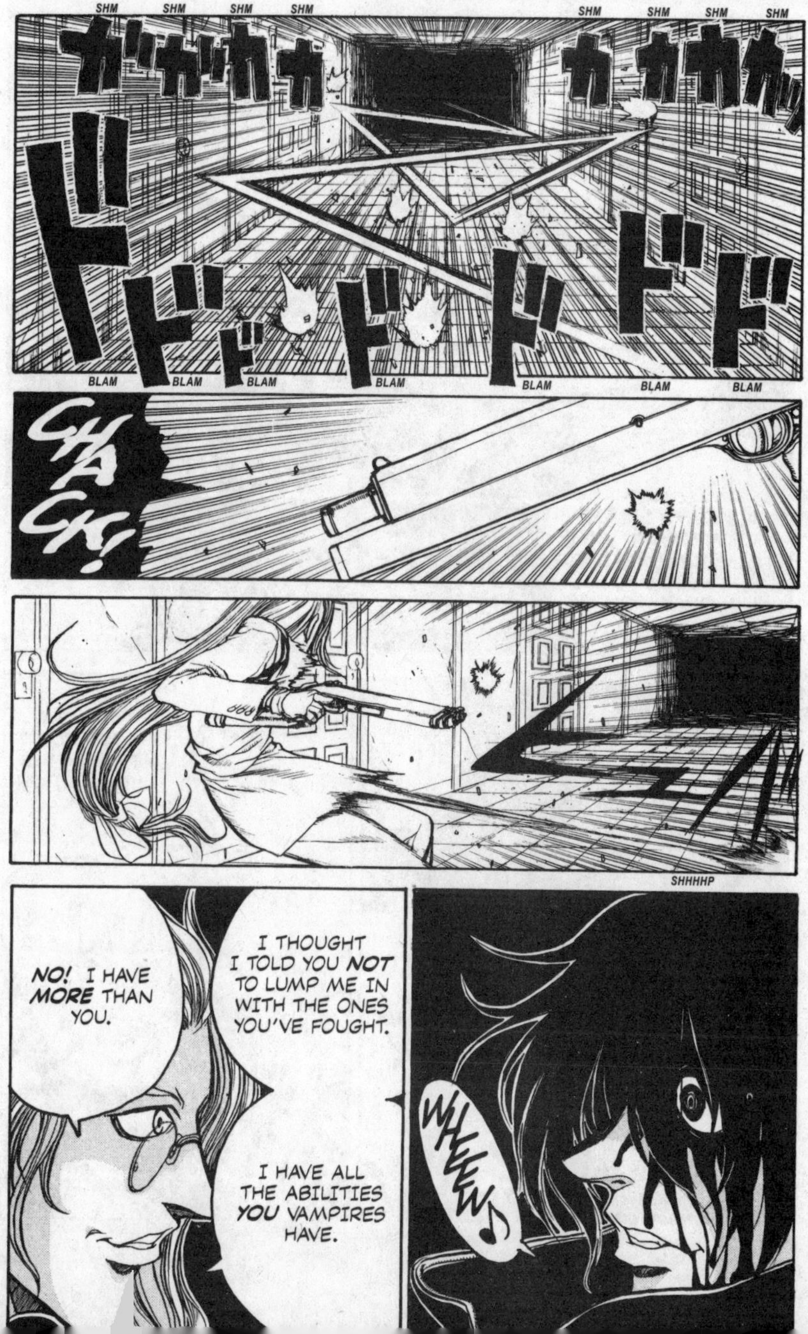
SHM SHM SHM SHM
SHM SHM SHM SHM
BLAM BLAM BLAM BLAM BLAM BLAM BLAM
CHACK!
SHHHHP
I THOUGHT I TOLD YOU *NOT* TO LUMP ME IN WITH THE ONES YOU'VE FOUGHT.
NO! I HAVE *MORE* THAN YOU.
I HAVE ALL THE ABILITIES *YOU* VAMPIRES HAVE.

WHO THE BLOODY HELL ARE YOU TWO? WHO'S MOVING YOU PAWNS ACROSS THE BOARD?
WHO TURNED YOU INTO VAMPIRES?!
JUST DON'T GET IT, DO YA GRAMPS?!
I ALREADY FUCKIN' TOLD YA, I'M OVERLORD JAN VALENTINE, LEADER OF THE HELLSING BEAT-DOWN SQUAD!!
LEER
COME OFF IT.
WHAT CAN YOU DO FROM DOWN THERE?
HYAHA HAA HA HAHA HAAA!
YOU REALLY ARE SENILE, MAN!
WE WERE BORN JUST TO KICK THE HELL OUT OF ALL YOU.
THEREFORE! ALL! YOU! BITCHES!
...CAN JUST CURL UP AND DIE!
Y'WANKER!
HNNNNN!

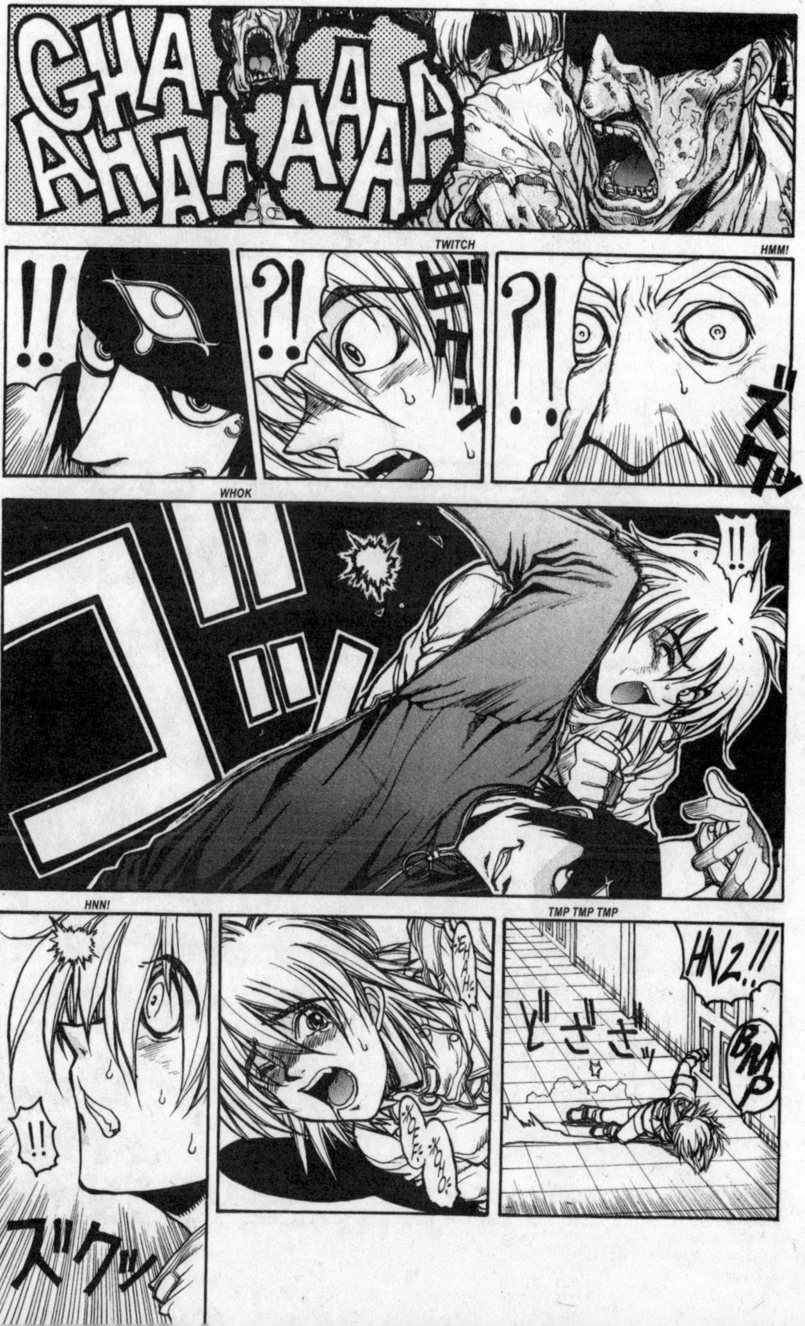
GHA
AHAHAAAAP
HMM!
?!!
ズグッ
TWITCH
?!
ビクッ
!!
WHOK
ゴッ
!!
TMP TMP TMP
BMP
どざざッ
HNN!
!!
ズグッ

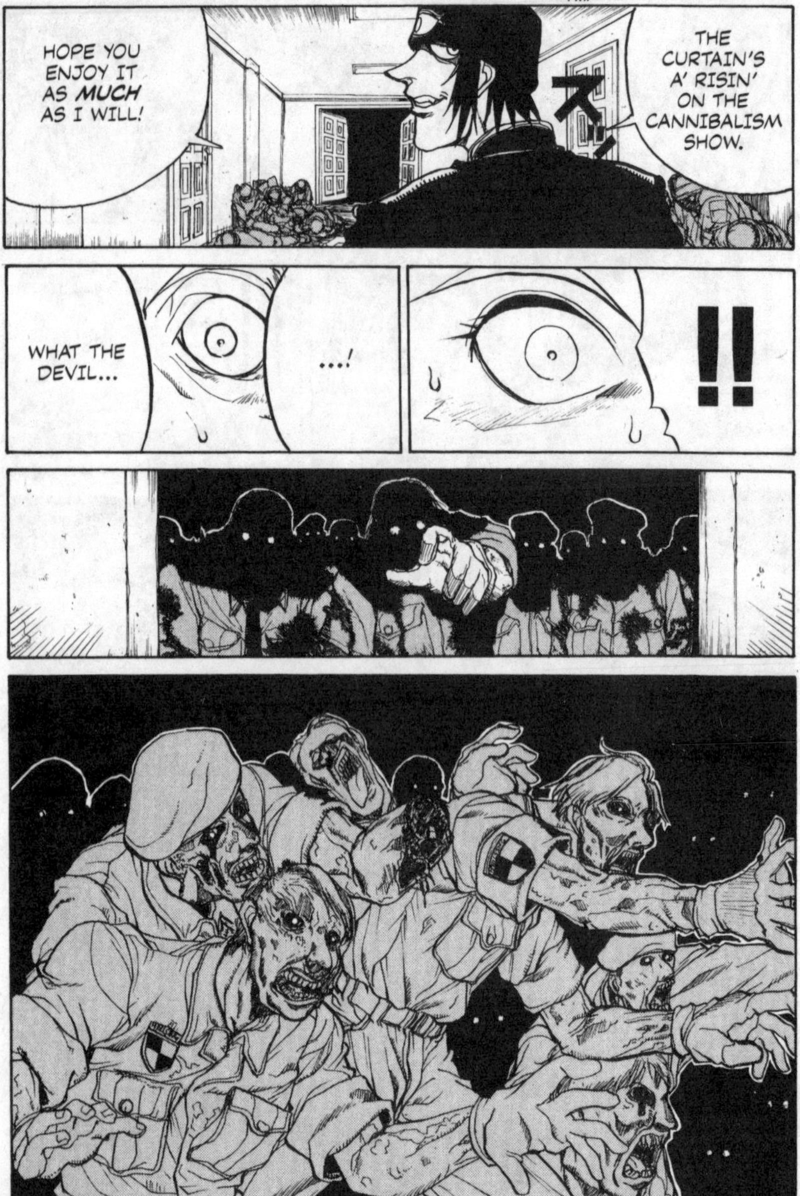
FWIP
THE CURTAIN'S A' RISIN' ON THE CANNIBALISM SHOW.
HOPE YOU ENJOY IT AS *MUCH* AS I WILL!
!!
...!
WHAT THE DEVIL...

SHFF
SHFF
SHFF
SHFF
THE PARTY!
...JUST GOT STARTED, YOU TWO!!
PAT
VMM
WHA--?!
SHMM
WHAT THE--?!
TMP

UH!
AGH!
AGHH!
AGHHHHH!
GRAB
GYAOHH!
ごちーん
WHAP
!!
EEEEEK!
ぬっはぁ
YEEE!
LUNGE

NO YOU DON'T!!
ヒュバッ
VSSSSH
キュラキュラキュラッ
ZHM ZHM ZHM
ビギッ
SHINK
HA!!
ブビチッ
ビチビチッ
ビチッ
RIP
SHRED
SHRRRIP
ブチブチ
ブチブチ
HA!!
HEEHEE HEE HEEHEE HEEHEE!
SHHHRIP
SHHHRIP

ガチャ
GCHAK
!!

WELCOME TO HELLSING.
WELCOME TO THE...
...ROUND TABLE COUNCIL.
shit
ドッ
BLAM
!!
ドウッ
BLAM

BLAM
BLAM
BLAM
ドドドン
AH
AAAAHA
バズ バズ
SSSMP
SSSMP
WHA--?
WHAT IN HELL...?!
バム
BAM

KBLAM
WHEEOO
SHAA
SHOO
HA!
KTAK
MAGNIFICENT.
EXCELLENT REFLEXIVE ABILITY.

OH, SAVE IT!!
THIS IS GREAT!! I HAVEN'T HAD THIS MUCH FUN IN AGES.
I CAN SEE THAT YOU'RE ABOVE EVEN A "CATEGORY A" VAMPIRE.
ZOOLLL

HE'S NOT EVEN TRYING TO DODGE MY SHOTS.
IS HE IMMORTAL?! NO! THERE'S NOTHING IMMORTAL IN THIS WORLD!!
HE ACTS LIKE HE'S FINE, BUT HE'S MORE HURT THAN I AM.
I CAN BEAT THE VAMPIRE ALUCARD!!
RELEASING CONTROL ART RESTRICTION TO LEVEL THREE, LEVEL TWO, LEVEL ONE.
SITUATION A. THE CROMWELL APPROVAL IS NOW IN EFFECT.
HOLD RELEASE UNTIL TARGET IS SILENCED.
NOW IT'S TIME TO TEACH YOU...
...HOW **REAL** VAMPIRES DO BATTLE.
ZWA
ZWA
ZWA
ZWA
ZWA
ZWA

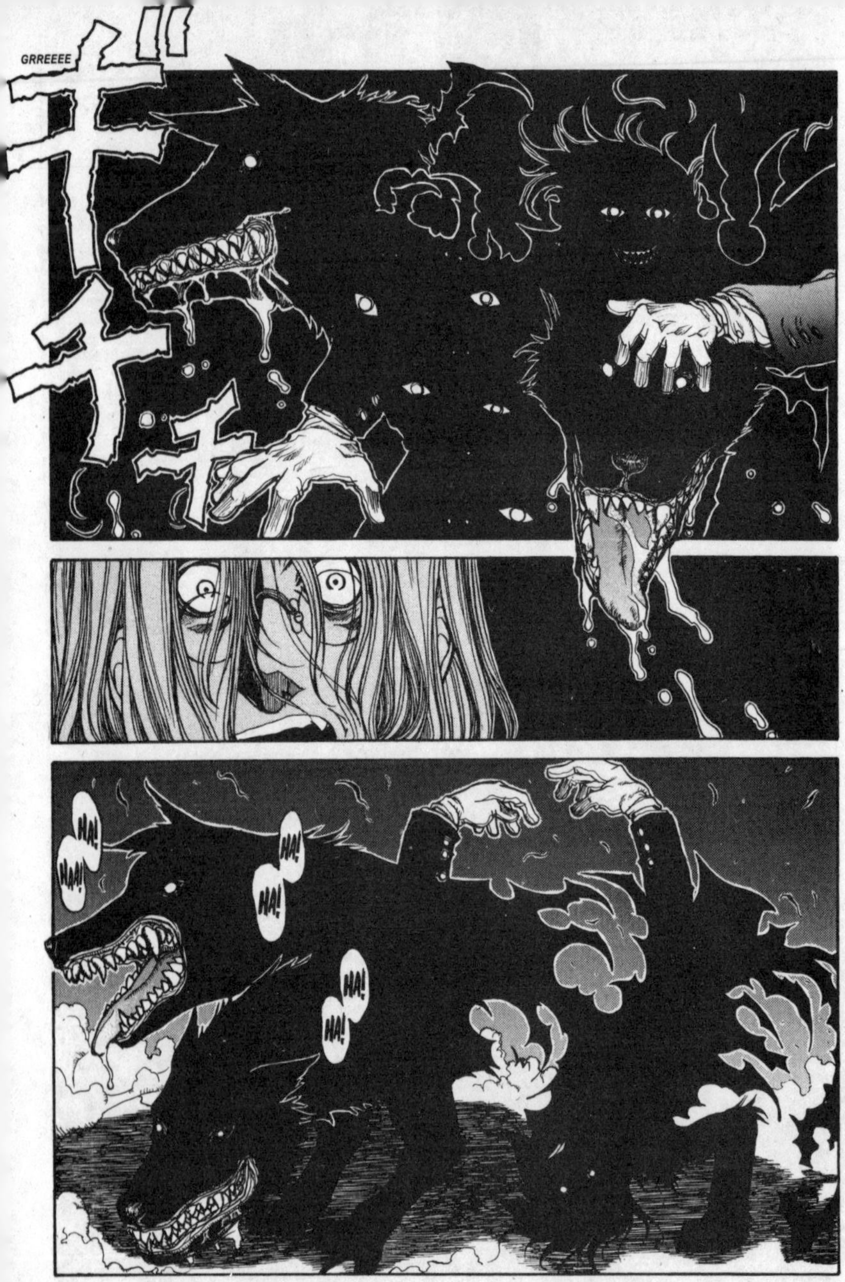
GRREEEE
ギギギ
HA!
HAA!
HA!
HA!
HA!
HA!

PLOP
ボタ
PLOP
ボタ
POT
NBEEEE
NBEEEE
NBEEEE
NBEEEE
NBEEEE
ゴボォオオ
ROWRRRRR

UWAH!
ガバアッ
ZHOOM
WHA!
AH!
UU!
ガチンガチン
SNAP
SNAP
CHIKA
CHIKA
CHIKA
CHIKA
RRRRRRN

AHH!
UNH!
NA!
OO!

バウッ
BLAM
ORDER 09 / END

ORDER 10

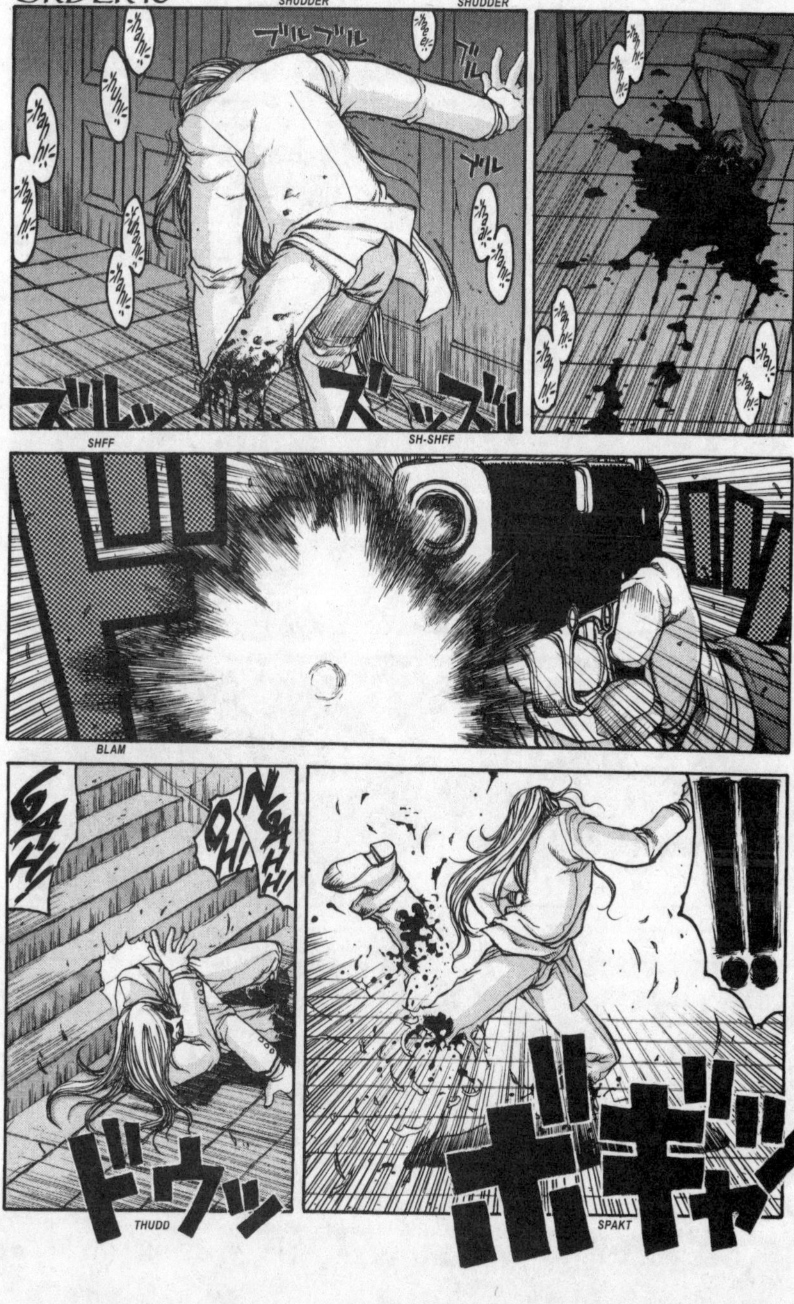
SHUDDER
SHUDDER
SHFF
SH-SHFF
BLAM
NGAHHH!
OH!
GAAH!
THUDD
SPAKT

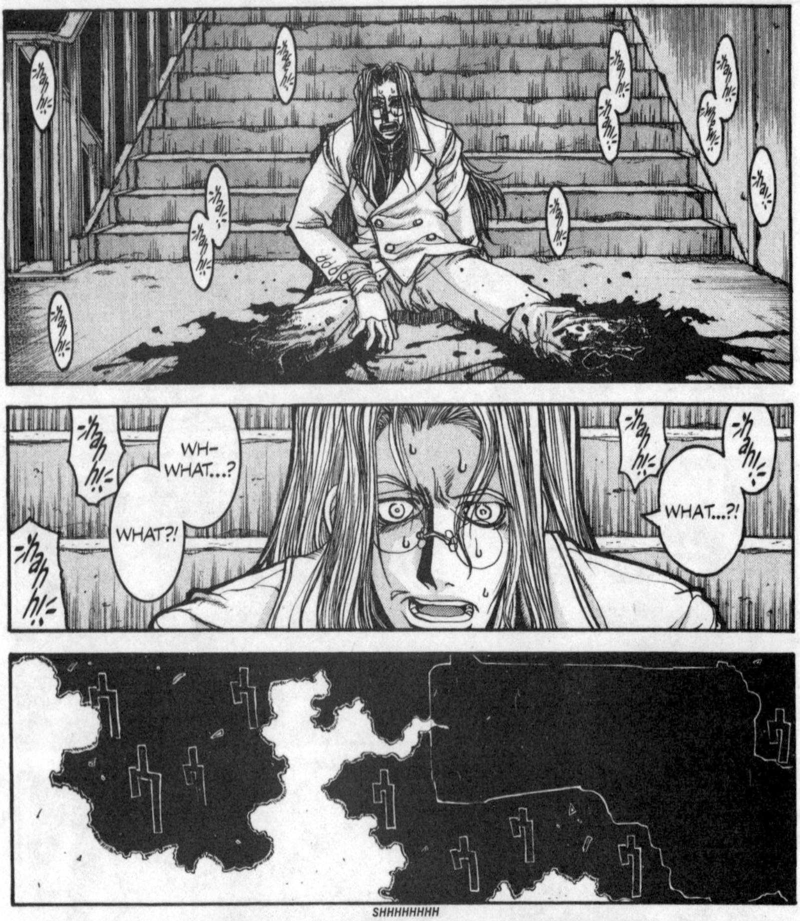
WHAT...?!
WH- WHAT...?
WHAT?!
SHHHHHHHH
WHAT... WHAT THE HELL...
...ARE YOU, ANYWAY?!

ORDER 10
デッドゾーン
DEAD ZONE ④

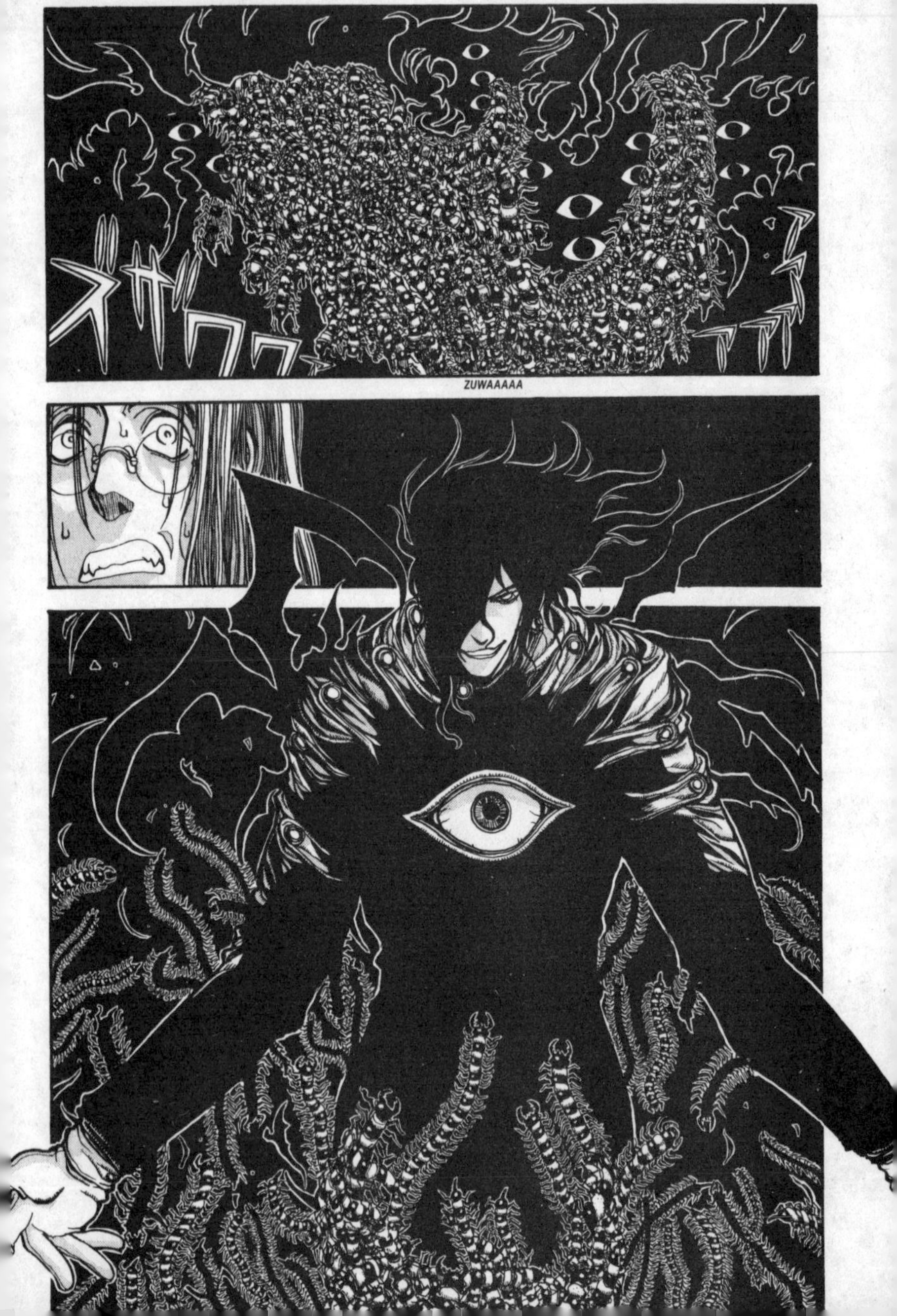
ZUWAAAAA

!!
YOU JUST HAD A COUPLA LEGS BLOWN OFF, THAT'S ALL.
WHAT'S THE MATTER?
COME GET ME!!
RECONSTRUCT YOUR LEGS AND STAND UP!! PICK UP YOUR GUNS AND FIGHT BACK!!
SUMMON YOUR FAMILIARS!! DISENGAGE YOUR BODY!!
G--! .... G--!
GODDAMN FREAK!!
THE NIGHT'S ONLY JUST BEGUN!! HERE'S WHERE IT GETS FUN!!
HURRY! HURRY HURRY!! HURRY HURRY HURRY!!!

OH. SO THAT'S WHAT YOU ARE, BOY.
A WORTHLESS, GOOD-FOR-NOTHING LUMP OF FLESH.
OH, PISS OFF, YOU LITTLE HELLSING TOY!!
YOU'RE JUST SOME VAMPIRE WHO'S THE ANGLICAN CHURCH'S DOG--
SILENCE!
THAT MAKES YOU DOG FOOD.

GROWRRRRRR
SHAK
OO!
OH!
AIEE!
WUOHH!
BLAM
BLAM
BLAM
BLAM
UNH!
AH!
OH!
OH!
AHH!
AHHH!

SHOMP
OEGO!
GEAH!
SO THAT WAS ALL YOU HAD AFTER ALL.
YOU WERE MORE A PIECE OF SHIT THAN A MAN.
NOW YOU CAN BE A PIECE OF DOG SHIT.
SNAP
CRNCH MNCH
CHMP
FROM THIS I CAN TELL HOW WEAK THE ONE UPSTAIRS IS...
YET IT SEEMS HE'S GIVING THEM QUITE A TOUGH TIME.
SHRMP
POK
CRACK
CHOMP
CHOMP
CHOMP

UWAH!
UWAH!
UWAH!
UWAHH!
ah!
Kwa!
Kfeh!
RASKK

NO...!
HOW COULD...!
MY MEN... EVEN MY STAFF ARE...
GHOULS...!!
WHOKK

KROSH
SERAAAAAS!!
!!
TAK
GSHH
HELLSING

HUAAAAAH
CHOK
KRRRNNNN
POLICE GIRL!!
KROSH
THAT'S ENOUGH!
SHFF
SERAS! STOP! YOU'VE DONE ENOUGH!
JUST...
JUST... STOP IT...

AH... AH.
AWAHHHHH!
KRAK
WHUNK

HEE HA... HEE HAAA.
ずるッ
KWA HA KHA! KHA HAA.
CHECKMATE, MY LAD.
NOT BAD, OLD DUDE.
YOU WON'T DIE FROM THAT ALONE.
BUT REST ASSURED, WE SHALL KILL YOU ONCE YOU TELL US WHOSE PAWN YOU ARE.
ガッ
SHFF
ALL Y'ALL'RE SOME *TRUE* DUMBASSES.

KATZ!
YO.
BITCH.
CHIK
KATZ KATZ
KATZ

NGAH!
GOHH!
BANG BANG BANG BANG BANG
ENOUGH OF YOUR PRATTLE.
I... AM QUITE PUT OUT.
HSSSSSSS
HUH! HUHEH. HUHE-HEHA.
HEEHA-HAHA HAHAHA.
SSSSSSSSM
WHO IN HELL ARE YOU PEOPLE?! HOW DID YOU MANAGE ALL THIS?!
WHO'S BEHIND THIS?!
ANSWER ME!!
HYAHAHA HAHAHA-HAH!
HAHA HAHA HAHAHA! HAA!

STOP LAUGHING!!
ANSWER ME!!
YOU PROBLY ALREADY KNOW THIS, BUT THAT MACHINE THING BURIED IN ME IS STILL SENDING INFO BACK TO THEM, EVEN NOW.
AFTER I SCREWED THIS UP AND TOLD YOU ALL THIS...
THEY KNOW THE ATTACK WENT TO SHIT... AND THEY HEAR THIS CONVERSATION, WORD FOR WORD!!
...YA THINK THEY'D LET ME LIVE?
SSSHAA

BROARRRRR
WHA--?!
?!
BROARRRR
ブオアアアア

HA A! A!
AH!
TOLD YA! HEE HA HAHA HAHA HAA!
AH!
HAHA HAHA!
HEEHEE HEEHAHA, I'LL TELL YOU DUMB SHITS!
JUST ONE THING THOUGH, HEEHEE HEEHEE!
ZHAAAAA
ザァァァァァ
!!
THRUST
HAPPY TRAILS, HOPE IT HELPS!!
BITCH!!

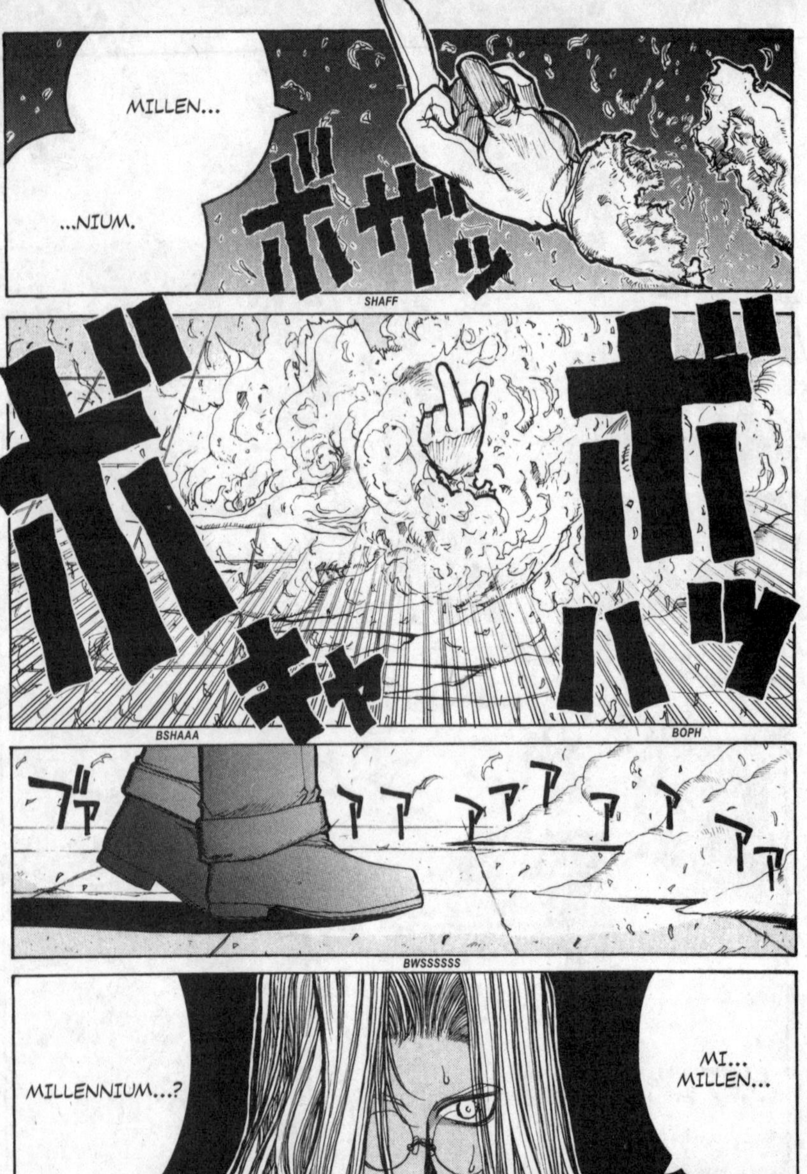
MILLEN...
...NIUM.
SHAFF
BOPH
BSHAAA
BWSSSSSS
MI... MILLEN...
MILLENNIUM...?

ARE YOU ALRIGHT, MY LADY?
YES, I...
BUT FORGET THAT. GO... PUT THEM OUT OF *THEIR* MISERY...
GHAAAU
HAA
YES...
NO, WALTER. THAT WON'T DO.
CHIK
THAT'S A COMMANDER'S JOB.
YOU SHOULD DO IT, SIR INTEGRA. *IT'S YOUR DUTY.*

SIR IRONS, I ENTREAT YOU NOT TO...
NO.
I WON'T ACCEPT THAT THIS WAS UNAVOIDABLE.
THERE SHOULD HAVE BEEN PROVISIONS OR A PLAN IN PLACE.
ALL RESPONSIBILITY LIES WITH YOU. YOU ARE THE COMMANDER, AFTER ALL.
AM I WRONG?
THE FACT THAT THESE MEN ARE DEAD OR UNDEAD IS ENTIRELY YOUR FAULT.
WALTER!!
SIR IRONS!!
ザアッ
ZAA
KAKZ
KAKZ
KAKZ
~~~!
~~~

KATZ
I WON'T ASK YOU TO FORGIVE ME.
IT'S ALL... MY FAULT.
CHAK
WALTER, LOOK INTO THIS MILLENNIUM THING.
WITH ALL SPEED AND THOROUGHNESS.
YES, SIR!
OF COURSE.
WE WILL REPAY THEM A BILLION-FOLD FOR THIS.
BLAMMMMM

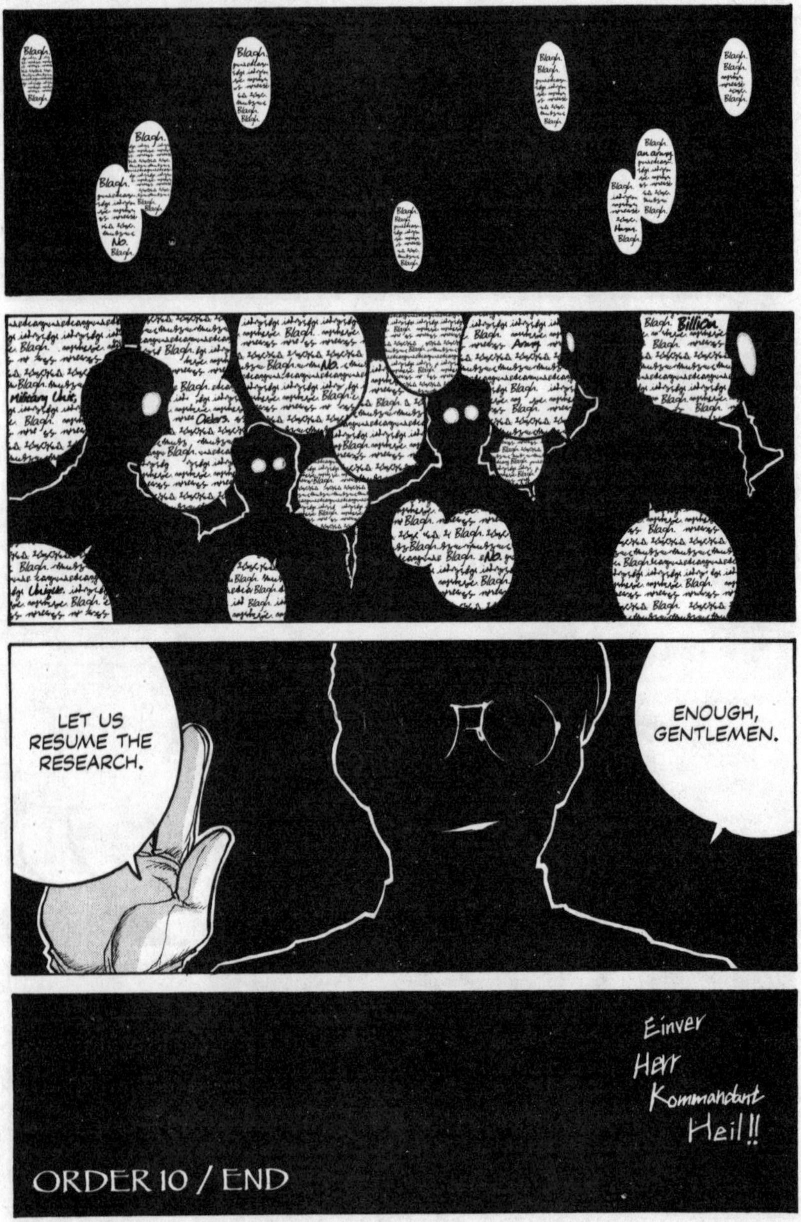
ENOUGH, GENTLEMEN.
LET US RESUME THE RESEARCH.
Einver Herr Kommandant Heil!!
ORDER 10 / END

SHHHHHHHHH
SHHHHHHHHHH
OUR FELLOW KNIGHTS WHO FELL IN THE SERVICE OF QUEEN, COUNTRY, AND THE PROTESTANT CHURCH...
WE SALUTE YOU!!
SALUTE

ORDER 11
バランス オブ パワー
BALANCE OF POWER ①

OF THE NINETY-SIX HELLSING LONDON BASE STAFF MEMBERS, ONLY TEN REMAIN ALIVE.
OF THOSE, EIGHT SURVIVED BECAUSE THEY WERE AWAY FROM BASE ON THAT DAY.
OUR FIRST URGENT BUSINESS IS THE REBUILDING OF HEADQUARTERS.
YOU FAILED TO INCLUDE SERAS AND ALUCARD IN THOSE NUMBERS.
IN OTHER WORDS, THE ONLY STAFF TO ACTUALLY SURVIVE THE ATTACK WERE THE TWO OF US, MY LADY.
...AH, OF COURSE.
PLAP
YES, AS FOR THOSE TWO...
...THEY'RE ALREADY DEAD, AFTER ALL.

HOW GOES THE INVESTIGATION INTO IT?
AH, YES.
"MILLENNIUM"...
...YOU MEAN.
THAT'S RIGHT.
IT HOLDS THE KEY TO THIS SITUATION.
ALL HANDS WE CAN SPARE ARE PRESENTLY LOOKING INTO IT.
VIA THE ROUND TABLE COUNCIL, MI-5 AND MI-6 ARE ALSO COOPERATING IN THE INVESTIGATION.
EVEN THE NATIONAL MUSEUM IS CURRENTLY SEARCHING ITS FULL ARCHIVES...
BUT NOTHING OF NOTE HAS BEEN FOUND.

THERE WERE SEVEN GROUPS DEVOTED TO SUCH THINGS AS THE OCCULT AND MILITARY STUDIES IN AMERICA, JAPAN, AND FRANCE.
AND ONE STAR WARS GROUP IN LOS ANGELES.
STAR WARS?
THE NAME OF HAN SOLO'S SHIP.
THE MILLENNIUM FALCON.
HUMPH!
WE MIGHT AS WELL HAVE NO INFORMATION AT ALL.
YES, MY APOLOGIES.
AT THIS POINT, WE KNOW NOTHING MORE THAN ITS FUNDAMENTAL MEANING.
FUNDAMENTAL...
...MEANING?
YES.
TEN CENTURIES, ONE THOUSAND YEARS.

PARDON?
NO, THERE IS ONE MORE.
HALF A CENTURY AGO.
THE GROUP THAT CHALLENGED THE ENTIRE WORLD FOR THE GLORY OF THE MILLENNIUM EMPIRE.
!!
THE NAZIS, THE THIRD REICH.
HITLER, GERMANY.

PROCEED WITH THE INVESTIGATION. OVERLOOK NOTHING!
UNDERSTOOD, MY LADY.
ALSO, REGARDING REPLACEMENT OF STAFF MEMBERS...
RECRUITING FROM THE BRITISH MILITARY WILL BE IMPOSSIBLE.
KRISH KRISH
WHY?
IT'S TOO UNNATURAL TO TRANSFER SO MANY.
THEREFORE...
REPORT OF
I EMPLOYED SOME PRO MERCENARIES.
MERCENARIES?
CAN WE RELY ON THEM?
WE CAN. THESE AREN'T JUST ANY MERCENARIES.
THEIR SOLE MOTIVATION IS MONEY.
THEY'RE PROFESSIONALS.
AS LONG AS THEY'RE PAID UNDER CONTRACT...
...THE WILD GEESE WILL NEVER BETRAY US.

WHAT'S ALL THIS THEN, CAPTAIN VERNEDEAD?
WHAT'S *WHAT?*
SOMETHING ABOUT US HAVING TO BE GUARDS OR SOMETHING?
ARE WE SOME RICH BLOKE'S PERSONAL ARMY?
NO, AND TRY NOT TO LET THIS *SPOOK* YOU.
OUR JOB THIS TIME...
...IS TO KILL OFF *MONSTERS!!*

KLAK
HAHAHA, C'MON!
IT'S TRUE.
ガッ
HA HA HA HA HA
BRITANICA COWBOYS
!!
YOUR ENEMIES ARE BLOOD SUCKING, AGELESS, IMMORTAL VAMPIRES.
WE CARRY GARLIC AND HOLY WATER, DRIVE WOODEN STAKES INTO THEIR HEARTS, AND CUT THEIR HEADS OFF.
THEN WE BURN THEIR CORPSES AND SCATTER THEIR ASHES AT A CROSSROAD. *THAT IS HOW WE WORK.*

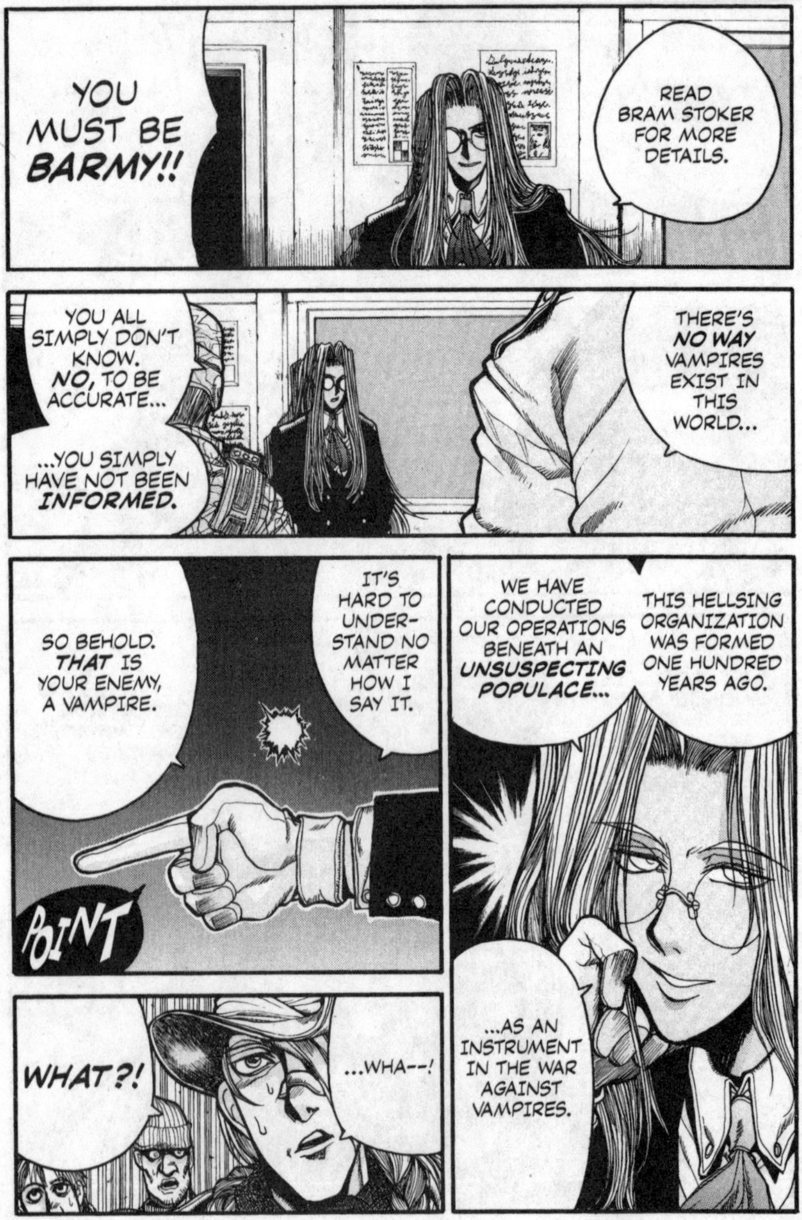
READ BRAM STOKER FOR MORE DETAILS.
YOU MUST BE BARMY!!
THERE'S NO WAY VAMPIRES EXIST IN THIS WORLD...
YOU ALL SIMPLY DON'T KNOW. NO, TO BE ACCURATE...
...YOU SIMPLY HAVE NOT BEEN INFORMED.
THIS HELLSING ORGANIZATION WAS FORMED ONE HUNDRED YEARS AGO.
WE HAVE CONDUCTED OUR OPERATIONS BENEATH AN UNSUSPECTING POPULACE...
...AS AN INSTRUMENT IN THE WAR AGAINST VAMPIRES.
IT'S HARD TO UNDER-STAND NO MATTER HOW I SAY IT.
SO BEHOLD. THAT IS YOUR ENEMY, A VAMPIRE.
POINT
...WHA--!
WHAT?!

WARRLL
WARRLL
WARRLL
YOU'RE...
...A VAMPIRE?
UH...
YEAH... SOME-THING OF THE SORT...
KIRAAN
MUMBLE MUMBLE
ざわ...ざわ...
PHAHA!
KHEHEH!
PFFF!
SIZZLE
メラメラメラメラ
I KNEW THEY'D LAUGH AT ME...
AND LAUGH THEY DO.
GO GO GO GO GO
SHOULDN'T MASTER BE HERE WITH ME?
NO.
HE WOULDN'T REST UNTIL THEY WERE ALL DEAD.

LIKE PIERRE TAKI a member of the techno band Denki Groove and a sometime actor.

I CHALLENGE YOU, CAPTAIN.
HN! GUOHH!
WHA...
WHAT?!
AND I'M ONLY ALLOWED TO FLICK MY FINGERS.
WHUMP
TOU.
ZHWP
GWOHHHH!
ZHWP
SHMP
BRASHH
GWOHH!
C-CAPTAIN!!
GYAHHHH!
SHE'S... A FREAK...!
CAN'T SEE HER AT ALL... CAN'T EVEN SENSE HER!
ALL SHE DID WAS FLICK ME, BUT MY HEAD'S SPINNIN'!
RIGHT, SO...
LIKE SHE SAID, I'M A VAMPIRE.
BRANDED A FREAK

YOU'RE REALLY... A VAMPIRE?
OF COURSE SHE IS.
ZULLLL
HOPPING DEMON
AMONG US, SHE'S LOWEST OF THE LOW...
...BUT SHE'S OBVIOUSLY A VAMPIRE.
GOGOGOGO SHAGEEE BUGOGOGO BTHUMP BTHUMP
UWAH HHH-AHH!
GYA-HAAA AAA!

BUDOGOGOGOGO
NOT MUCH IN THE WAY OF GUTS.
WILL THEY BE OF ANY USE TO US?
ALUCARD!!
CHATTA CHATTA CHATTA AIIEEEEEE
MY HUMBLE APOLOGIES, MY LADY.
I TRIED TO STOP HIM...
KATZ
WALTER...
THEY'LL BE GUARDING MY BED.
I WANT TO SEE WHAT MANNER OF MEN THEY ARE.
....
....
THAT ASIDE, MY LADY.
WHAT IS IT?

ZZZP
ZA
THIS WAS SENT TO US.
ズパッ
ザッ
A LETTER...?
NOTICE THE SENDER, IF YOU WOULD.
!!
YES.
GRIN
VATICAN SECTION XIII...
THE ISCARIOT AGENCY?!
ORDER 11 / END

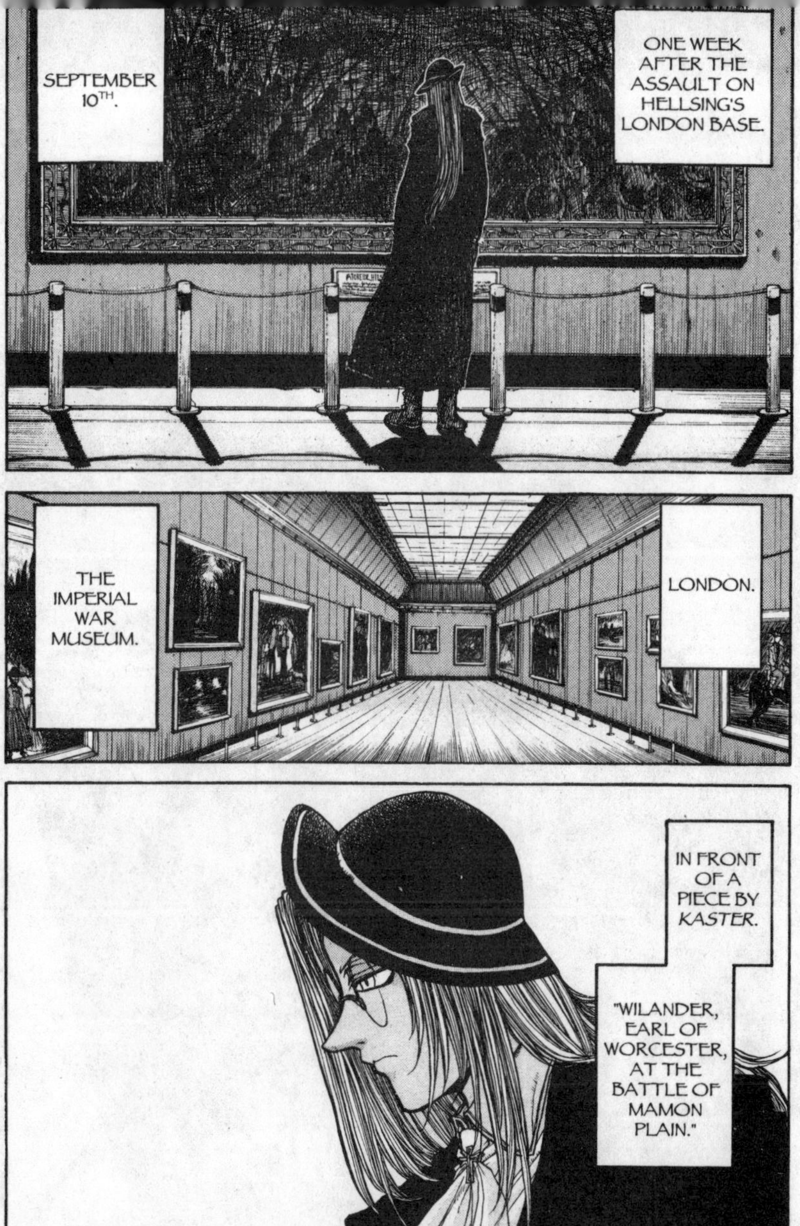
ONE WEEK AFTER THE ASSAULT ON HELLSING'S LONDON BASE.
SEPTEMBER 10TH.
LONDON.
THE IMPERIAL WAR MUSEUM.
IN FRONT OF A PIECE BY *KASTER*.
"WILANDER, EARL OF WORCESTER, AT THE BATTLE OF MAMON PLAIN."

ORDER 12
バランス
BALANCE
オブ パワー
OF POWER②

"SIR INTEGRA WINGATES HELLSING, LEADER OF THE HELLSING ORGANIZATION,
"HOW WOULD YOU LIKE TO ENJOY AN ART MUSEUM TOGETHER THIS FINE AUTUMN?
"I SHALL AWAIT YOU AT 3PM ON THE 10TH AT THE FOLLOWING PLACE...
"ENRICO MAXWELL, HEAD OF VATICAN SECTION XIII, THE ISCARIOT AGENCY."
WHAT TIME IS IT, WALTER?
RIGHT.
IT IS JUST ABOUT THREE O'CLOCK.
カパッ
KPOK
...THEY INVITED US AND NOW ***THEY'RE*** LATE.
I DOUBT THIS...
...BUT THEY MAY HAVE ***LURED*** US OUT INTO A TRAP.
NO. REGARDLESS OF ***WHO*** AND ***WHAT*** THEY ARE...
...I DO NOT THINK THEY WOULD TRY ANYTHING IN PUBLIC, BROAD DAYLIGHT, AND IN THE MIDDLE OF HOSTILE TERRITORY.

I TELL YOU, THAT MONOPHONE WAS SIMPLY AMAZING.
I LEAVE IT TO THE IMPERIAL WAR MUSEUM TO DO SUCH QUALITY RESTORATION.
INDEED, YOU ARE QUITE CORRECT.
CERTAINLY A LOT OF PLANES HERE, TOO.
THAT WAS THE FIRST TIME I'VE EVER SEEN A ZERO!! WHAT BEAUTIFUL FORM.
YES, YES.
AH.
OH MY, PERHAPS WE'RE LATE.
SO IT APPEARS.

HELLO, HELLO.
IT SEEMS I'VE KEPT YOU WAITING.
THAT'S CLOSE ENOUGH.
KATZ KATZ KATZ KATZ KATZ
WHAT IN THE WORLD DOES THE VATICAN WANT?
MOREOVER, THE ANNIHILATION AGENCY ISCARIOT, A NAME TO HUSH A CRYING CHILD!
AHH, THIS WILL NOT DO.
YOU SEEM TO HOLD QUITE THE GRUDGE.
FIRST, I SHOULD GREET YOU.
MY NAME IS MAXWELL, AND I AM THE HEAD OF ISCARIOT.
PLEASED TO MAKE YOUR ACQUAINTANCE.

WHAT'S YOUR BUSINESS HERE?!
SELF-INTRODUCTIONS ARE MEANINGLESS!!
PLEASE, THERE IS NO NEED FOR SUCH A TONE.
WE ARE NOT HERE TO FIGHT WITH YOU TODAY.
YOU EXPECT ME TO BELIEVE THAT?!
YOU DISPATCHED YOUR AGENT ANDERSON TO BADRICK IN NORTH IRELAND IN GRAVE VIOLATION OF TREATY!
HE MURDERED TWO OF OUR MEN!!
....
....
AND HE WAS A MERE STEP AWAY FROM KILLING ME AS WELL!
DON'T TELL ME YOU'VE FORGOT-TEN!!

SO, WHAT OF IT?!
!
...I BEG YOUR PARDON?!
WE COME TO YOU HUMBLY AND YOU THROW IT IN OUR FACES.
ガッ
KATZ
I COULDN'T CARE LESS IF TWO OR TWO BILLION OF YOU DAMNED PROTESTANT SWABS HAVE DIED.
DO YOU THINK I WOULD BOTHER TALKING TO THE LIKES OF YOU FILTH WERE IT NOT HIS HOLINESS' DIRECT ORDER?
SO SHUT YOUR MOUTH AND LISTEN WELL.
YOU PROTESTANT SOW.

SOW?!
!!
THAT'S WHAT I'D EXPECT FROM THE INFAMOUS SECTION XIII.
NOTHING EVER CHANGES.
NOTHING'S EVER CHANGED IN ROME THESE PAST 2000 YEARS.
ALWAYS TRYING TO IMPOSE THEIR PEACE AND LAWS ON EVERYONE ELSE.
THOSE AT THE TOP SQUELCHING ANY WHO OPPOSE THEIR POWER.
THE NOSFERATU ALUCARD.
HELLSING'S TRASHMAN!! THE KILLER JOKER!!

I'VE NOT SEEN YOU IN THE FLESH.
GREETINGS, ALUCARD.
GREETINGS, MAXWELL.
AND FAREWELL.
YOU.
YOU JUST CALLED MY MASTER A SOW.
DON'T THINK THAT I'LL LET YOU LEAVE THIS COUNTRY ALIVE.
YOU'RE AS GOOD AS DEAD, HUMAN!!

WE WILL NEVER GET ANYWHERE WITH SUCH A SCARY BODYGUARD WAVING A GUN AROUND.
OHH, HOW FRIGHTENING.
I SAY IT AGAIN, WE ARE HERE SIMPLY TO SPEAK WITH YOU.
BUT IF THAT IS HOW YOU WANT IT...
...WE MUST FOLLOW SUIT...
...IN ORDER FOR US TO RETAIN EQUAL FOOTING.
!!
AAAANDERSON!

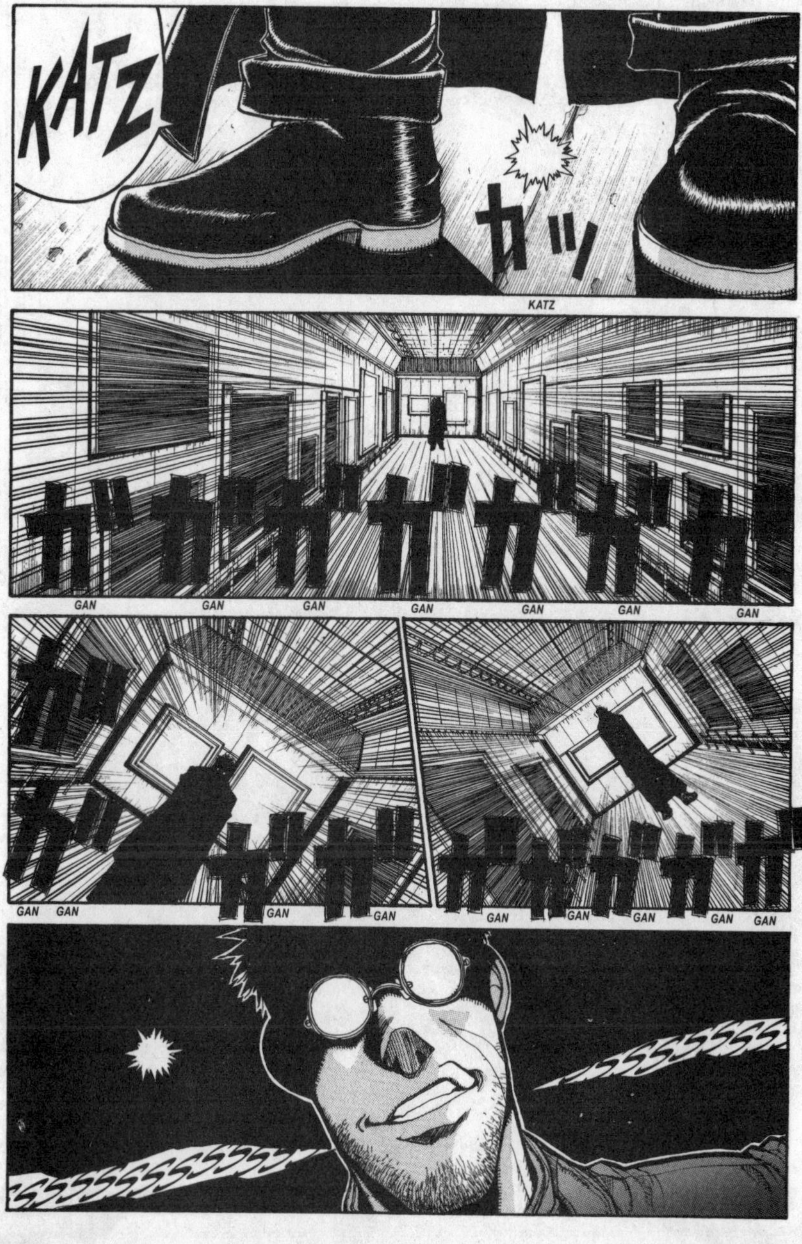
KATZ
カッ
KATZ
GAN
GAN
GAN
GAN
GAN
GAN
GAN
GAN
GAN
GAN
GAN
GAN
GAN
GAN
GAN
GAN
GAN

ASK O' ME, AND AH SHALL GIE THEE THE HEATHEN FOR THINE INHERITANCE, AND THE UTMOST PARTS O' THE EARTH FOR THY POSSESSION.
THOU SHALT BREAK THEM WI' AE ROD O' IRON; THOU SHALT DASH THEM IN PIECES LIKE AE POTTER'S VESSEL.
カッカッ
KATZ KATZ
カッカッ
KATZ KATZ
!!
BE WISE NOO THEREFORE, O' YE KINGS: BE INSTRUCTED, YE JUDGES O' THE EARTH.
SERVE THE LAIRD WI' FEAR, AND REJOICE WI' TREMBLING. KISS THE SON, LEST HE BE ANGRY, AND YE PERISH FAE THE WAY,
WHEN HIS WRATH IS KINDLED BUT AE LITTLE. BLESSED ARE A' THEY THON PUT THEIR TRUST IN HIM.
カッカッカッ
KATZ KATZ KATZ
N--!
NO!
STOP IT, ANDERSON!!
?!
A' WILL BE SETTLED WI JUST A BLOW.
WHIT GOOD'S ISCARIOT, OR THE VATICAN, IF WE LET AN ENEMY SLIP OOT O' OOR GRASP?!
カッカッカッカッ
KATZ KATZ KATZ KATZ
THERE IS NO NEED FOR VIOLENCE!!
STOP THIS!!
HE'S LOST ALL CONTROL NOW THAT HE'S SEEN YOU.
GO, LEAVE THIS PLACE FOR NOW! WE'LL TRY ONCE AGAIN TO--
!!

Hellsing Arm 454 Casull
AUTO

HEHEHEH! HEHEHE-HEHEH.
YES!! LET US KILL, JUDAS PRIEST!
HAHAAH, HAHAHA-HAHAHH.
JUS LIKE LAST TIME, VAMPIRE.
GCHANK
!!
NO!!
N--!

ALL RIGHT THEN, EVERY-ONE!
HERE WE HAVE THE PAINTING GALLERY!
NORTH KASUKABE ELDERLY SOCIETY
BANNN
SHFF
SHFF
SHFF
SHFF
GEHEH!
NORTH KASUKABE ELDERLY SOCIETY
TRMP TRMP
TRMP
TRMP
RIGHT THIS WAY, JAPANESE FOLLLKS!
BTHMP
BTHMP
BTHMP
BTHMP
POLICE GIRL
-cough- -cough- <sunflowers, hm?>
SHFF
SHFF
SHFF
SHFF
SHFF
SHFF

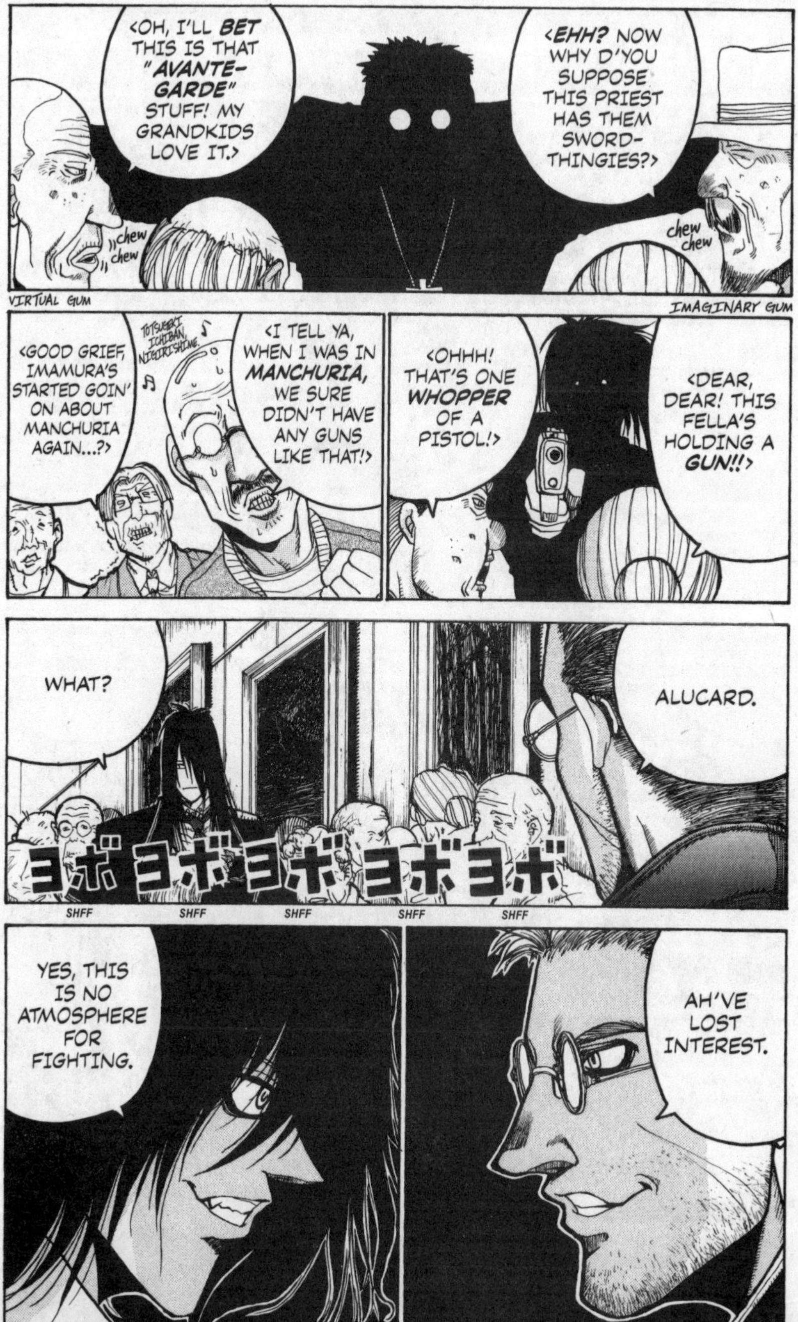
<EHH? NOW WHY D'YOU SUPPOSE THIS PRIEST HAS THEM SWORD-THINGIES?>
chew chew
<OH, I'LL BET THIS IS THAT "AVANTE-GARDE" STUFF! MY GRANDKIDS LOVE IT.>
chew chew
IMAGINARY GUM
VIRTUAL GUM
<DEAR, DEAR! THIS FELLA'S HOLDING A GUN!!>
<OHHH! THAT'S ONE WHOPPER OF A PISTOL!>
<I TELL YA, WHEN I WAS IN MANCHURIA, WE SURE DIDN'T HAVE ANY GUNS LIKE THAT!>
TOTSUGEKI ICHIBAN, NIGIRISHIME.
<GOOD GRIEF, IMAMURA'S STARTED GOIN' ON ABOUT MANCHURIA AGAIN...?>
ALUCARD.
WHAT?
ヨボヨボヨボヨボヨボ
SHFF SHFF SHFF SHFF SHFF
AH'VE LOST INTEREST.
YES, THIS IS NO ATMOSPHERE FOR FIGHTING.

I'M GOING BACK TO BED.
WHA--?!
KATZ
KATZ
AND YOUR GUARD DUTY?
WITH ANDERSON GONE, OLD WALTER WILL BE MORE THAN SUFFICIENT ALONE.
NOW THEN, HERE WE HAVE...
BEING UP ALL DAY MAKES ME SLEEPY.
AH'LL BE HEADING BACK TAE ROME AFORE YE.
KATZ
KATZ
KATZ
I SEE.
KATZ
THIS IS AE NICE MUSEUM.
LET'S BRING THE CHILDREN FAE THE ORPHANAGE NEXT TIME.
BY ALL MEANS.
HAHHH
NEXT TIME AH *KILL* HIM.
AH SWEAR IT.

WHEW.
IT IS DIFFICULT FOR US TO TALK HERE.
WHY DON'T WE CONTINUE THIS IN THE CAFETERIA OUTSIDE?
HM?
ガヤガヤガヤガヤ
MURMUR
MURMUR
MURMUR
MURMUR
I SEEM TO KEEP REPEATING MYSELF...
BUT I HAVE COME HERE TO TALK.
....
....
...VERY WELL.
WE WILL BOTH LEAVE OUR DREADFUL SUBORDINATES BEHIND.
RIGHT? SWINE?
JOLLY GOOD SHOW!!
ビシッ
FWIP
THANK YOU VERY MUCH!!
ビシッ
FWIP
PAYBACK FOR EARLIER.
FAIR ENOUGH, I'LL ENDURE IT!!
ハーーー
WHEW

KREE
WE KNOW OF YOUR SITUATION.
YOU CAME UNDER ATTACK BY ORGANIZED GHOULS AND ARE ON THE BRINK OF DESTRUCTION.
AND BASED ON WHAT WE HAVE HEARD...
...YOU ARE CONDUCTING A FRANTIC SEARCH.

ALSO, YOU HAVE NOT FOUND WHAT YOU SEARCH FOR.
INDEED, THAT IS THE CASE.
"MILLENNIUM"...
...RIGHT?
.....
.....

THIS IS, HOW TO SAY, VERY TOP-SECRET,
BUT WE POSSESS A PIECE OF INFORMATION ABOUT MILLENNIUM.
WANT ME TO TELL YOU? REALLY?
IS THAT WHAT YOU WISH? IS IT REALLY?
LEER
WHAT DO YOU MEAN TO SAY?

IT IS UNHEARD OF FOR US TO OFFER ASSISTANCE TO YOU INFERNAL PROTESTANTS.
BUT WE THOUGHT WE WOULD REPAY THE DEBT WE OWED YOU FROM THAT TREATY VIOLATION IN BADRICK.
AND WE WANT YOU TO RECOGNIZE THIS.
FINE.
...YOU HAVE OUR CONSENT.
BUT THAT'S NOT QUITE ENOUGH.
NOT ENOUGH FOR ME TO TELL YOU.
WHAT?

THERE IS AN IMPORANT WORD REQUIRED WHEN YOU ASK SOMETHING OF SOMEONE.
"PLEASE"!
NOW YOU'RE TRYING TO TAKE ADVANTAGE OF US!
WALTER!!
WE CAN ACQUIRE TOP-SECRET VATICAN INFO WITH JUST ONE WORD.
IT'S NOT A BAD DEAL.
BESIDES, WE ARE NOT IN A POSITION RIGHT NOW TO BE CHOOSY.
I WILL EVEN DRAW STRAWS AT THIS POINT.
MY LADY...
ニヤリ
GRIN

PLEASE.
I DON'T CARE HOW SMALL A THING IT IS. WOULD YOU TELL ME?
DIRECTOR OF THE SPECIAL AGENCY ISCARIOT, VATICAN SECTION XIII OF THE ROMAN CATHOLIC CHURCH.
FATHER MAXWELL.
OKAY! OKAY!! AGREED!!
DIRECTOR OF HELLSING, THE ORDER OF BRITISH PROTESTANT KNIGHTS, SIR INTEGRAL FAIRBROOK WINGATES HELLSING.

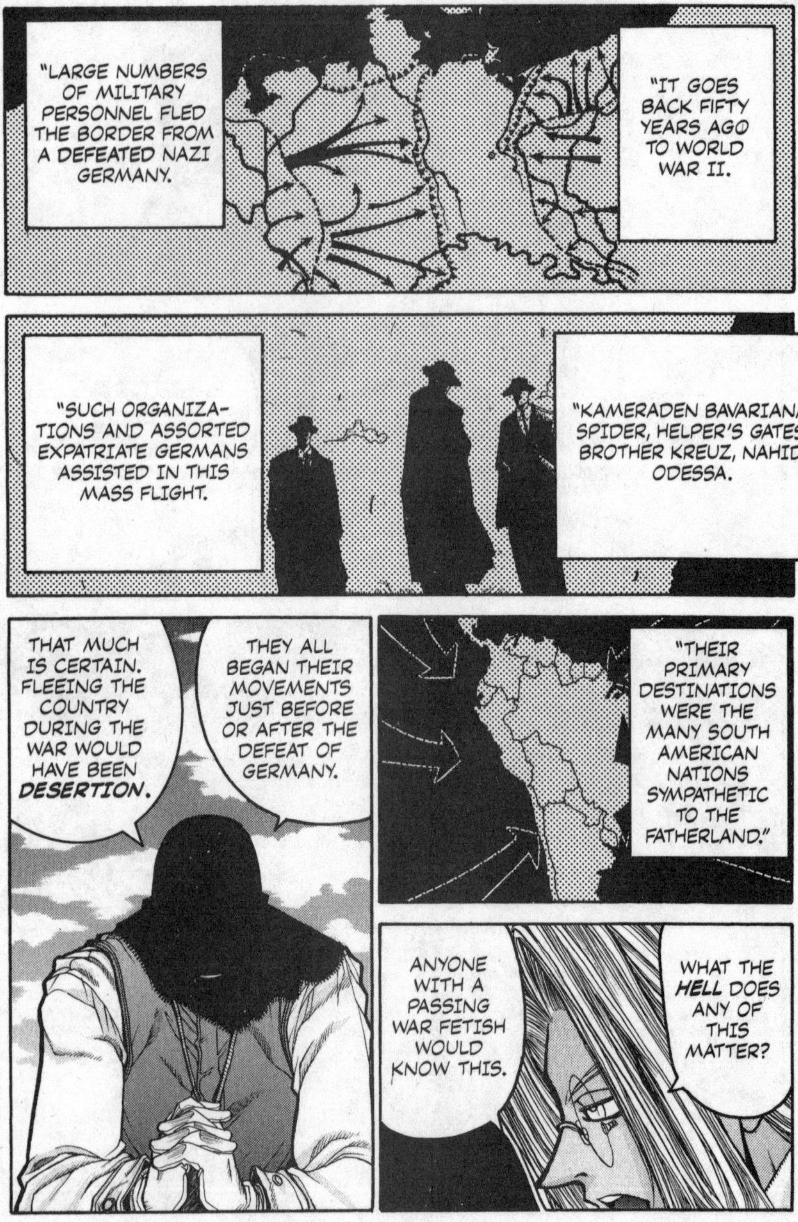
"IT GOES BACK FIFTY YEARS AGO TO WORLD WAR II.
"LARGE NUMBERS OF MILITARY PERSONNEL FLED THE BORDER FROM A DEFEATED NAZI GERMANY.
"SUCH ORGANIZA-TIONS AND ASSORTED EXPATRIATE GERMANS ASSISTED IN THIS MASS FLIGHT.
"KAMERADEN BAVARIANA, SPIDER, HELPER'S GATES, BROTHER KREUZ, NAHID, ODESSA.
THAT MUCH IS CERTAIN. FLEEING THE COUNTRY DURING THE WAR WOULD HAVE BEEN ***DESERTION***.
THEY ALL BEGAN THEIR MOVEMENTS JUST BEFORE OR AFTER THE DEFEAT OF GERMANY.
"THEIR PRIMARY DESTINATIONS WERE THE MANY SOUTH AMERICAN NATIONS SYMPATHETIC TO THE FATHERLAND."
ANYONE WITH A PASSING WAR FETISH WOULD KNOW THIS.
WHAT THE ***HELL*** DOES ANY OF THIS MATTER?

Bericht Jahrhundert
THE MILLENNIUM WE KNOW IS THE NAME OF A PROJECT AND A MILITARY UNIT.
THEY ARE THE ONES WHO CARRY OUT THE HIGHLY CLASSIFIED TRANSFER OF RESOURCES AND PERSONNEL FOR THE NAZIS.
THIS MILLENNIUM HAS BEEN WORKING DILIGENTLY SINCE THE INITIAL STAGES OF THE WAR.
バサッ
RUSTLE
THEY RAN AROUND OCCUPIED GERMANY FALSIFYING DOCUMENTS WHILE EXPANDING THEIR RESOURCES AND GATHERING PROMISING MEN OF TALENT.
THEY TRANSPORTED EVERYTHING TO SOUTH AMERICA... CONFISCATED JEWISH PROPERTY, WORKS OF ART, PRECIOUS METALS, FOREIGN CURRENCY, VALUABLE SECURITIES, AND SO ON.
FROM THE SMALLEST GOLD TOOTH TO THE LARGEST SUBMARINE.

YOU WISH TO KNOW HOW WE KNOW, DO YOU?
BECAUSE THE VATICAN HELPED!
CONSIDERABLY!

IT SEEMS ZEY'VE FINALLY DISCOVERED US.
MILLENNIUM.
DISCOVERED?
NONSENSE, THEY STILL DO NOT REALIZE A THING.

SHALL VE ACCELERATE OUR OPERATIONS?
NO, NOT YET.
ACTUALLY, I VOULD LIKE SOME MORE TEA.
....
....
THIS PROMISES TO BE ENJOYABLE, MEIN FÜHRER.
YES, WERY. WERY ENJOYABLE.
IT VILL BE CONFLICT. THINK ABOUT IT.
I'M CERTAIN IT VILL BE A CONFLICT STAINED VITH MUCH BLOOD. MAGNIFICENT, ISN'T IT? CONFLICT...
ORDER 12 / END

- YEAHHH. CHINKO CHINKO! (MY GREETING) GOOD EVENING. THIS IS KOHTA HIRANO. AND SO HERE IT IS FINALLY, HELLSING VOLUME 2. IT'S LIKE, "PUB-LIIIIISH!!" OR SOMETHING. IT ENDED UP TAKING MORE THAN A WHOLE YEAR TO GET IT RELEASED. AND IT'S LEFT ME EXHAUSTED. IT WAS ROUGH! I'M ALL WORN OUT. I'M KAORU KUROKI. IT'S A SEXUAL RELEASE. TOOOOT TOOOOOT (PROUDLY SHOWING OFF HER ARMPITS WHILE PLAYING A LITTLE CONCH SHELL) TOOOOT TOOOOT TOOOOT TOOOOT TOOOOT TOOOT

  *note: Kaoru Kuroki was an actress in the '80s, famous for not shaving her armpits. She was also known to talk about the idea of sexual release a lot.

- AND SO, CHARACTERS FROM MY ADULT BOOKS WILL SHOW UP. NAZIS WILL SHOW UP. SINCE VOLUME 1 I'VE BEEN ABLE TO DO ABSOLUTELY WHATEVER I PLEASE, BUT YOU KNOW, IT'S KIND OF LIKE SOME RAMEN SHOP OWNED AND RUN BY ONE GUY AND THE RAMEN IS TERRRRIBLE. NO MATTER WHAT ANYONE SAYS HE DOESN'T GIVE THEM THE TIME OF DAY AND KEEPS SERVING CRAPULENT RAMEN. SO ALL I CAN SAY IS I'M SORRY IT ALL SEEMS SO WEIRD AND DARK.

- THERE WAS A LOT OF FOCUS ON OLD MEN IN THIS VOLUME AND IT PROBABLY SEEMS FISHY AND UNBALANCED TO THE READERS. ALL I CAN SAY IS I'M SORRY.

- IN ANY CASE, FROM HERE ON THE STORY WILL GO ON "DAAAARA DAAAARA," AND IT'D MAKE ME HAPPY IF ALL OF YOU READ IT "DAAAARA DAAAARA." BUT THEN I GUESS IT'S ALREADY THAT WAY ANYWAY. DARAAAA DARAAAA. MIDARA-AAA MIDARAAAA! NOOO NOOO NOOO NOOO! IT'S TEN DARAAAA (SOUNDING LIKE TAKAYANAGI FROM SMAP).

  *note: you're going to have to figure this stuff out on your own!

- ZZ GUNDAM IS PRETTY COOL...
  I WONDER IF ROUX LOUKA WOULD BE
  WILLING TO MARRY ME...

- MAYBE I WISH MRS. DEVI WOULD JUST DIE.
  MARIANNE, TOO.

  *note: Two Japanese celebrities who have been known to hold grudges against each other. Think afternoon talk-show fare.

~THE IDIOT BROTHERS~

OLDER CHOSUKE →

← YOUNGER KOJI

*note: Koji and Chosuke are the names of two comedians who used to have a show where they pretended to be idiot brothers.

(USELESS) CHARACTER DESCRIPTIONS

■ JAN VALENTINE

HE GOT BURNED TO A CRISP. BWOOOSH. I **DREW** ALL THOSE PIERCINGS AND EVEN I THOUGHT THEY LOOKED PAINFUL. I KEPT THINKING, "WHO ARE YOU, KAKIHARA?!" OF COURSE, IF THEY MISS IT'LL BE A COCK PIERCING. TWO OF THEM, EVEN. "AT THIS POINT, THE DOG'S THE ONLY ONE NOT FREAKIN' OUT." GINYAAA! **GOODBYE,** JAN VALENTINE.

*note: Kakihara is a character from the movie "Ichi the Killer," and has lots of facial metal.

■ LUKE VALENTINE

GUESS HE WAS TOO MUCH FORM OVER FUNCTION. HE DOESN'T DESERVE TO WEAR ROUND GLASSES. AND YOU KNOW, THAT'S IT! IN TERMS OF ***SAINT SEIYA***, HE'S KIND OF LIKE CANCER DEATHMASK I GUESS. "SEKISHIKI MEIKAI HAAAA!" "I'M DROPPING YOU STRAIGHT DOWN THE YOMOTSU HIRASAKA!" GYAPIII! **GOODBYE,** LUKE VALENTINE.

*note: The Japanese attack shouted out above translates to "Cancer Hades Wave." The Yomotsu Hirasaka is a cliff or slope said to be on the pathway to Hades in Japanese mythology. This is an actual scene in the ***Saint Seiya*** series.

■ DIRECTOR MAXWELL

HE ALSO APPEARED IN "CROSS FIRE," BUT HE LOOKED TOO MUCH LIKE INTEGRA SO I SLICKED HIS HAIR BACK. ALSO HAD HIM LOSE HIS GLASSES. THEN, SAY WHAT?! HE'S LIKE A WHOLE OTHER CHARACTER. IF I DON'T DO ANYTHING TO DIFFERENTIATE MY CHARACTERS, IT LEADS TO REALIZATION. LETDOWN. DISAPPOINTMENT. INCONTINENCE. BLOODY STOOL. FAINTING. DEATH. HEAVEN. REINCARNATION. HI, I'M BACK.

■ DARK SHADOWS MAN

HE'S A **VILLAIN** SO HE GETS LOTS OF DARK SHADING.

◀ CROSS FIRE PART 2...COMMONLY KNOWN AS "ROSS; FA" FOR SHORT.

NOT ENOUGH! THERE AREN'T ENOUGH PAGES!! AND SO, CONTINUING ON FROM VOLUME 1, THIS IS PART 2 OF THE STORY. HERE FOLLOWS THE SECOND ONE-SHOT INSTALLMENT IN WHICH MEMBERS OF THE VATICAN SPECIALIZED SECRET AGENCY SECTION XIII ISCARIOT ARE THE MAIN CHARACTERS. THE ART AND STORY ARE BOTH KIND OF ROUGH AND CRUDE SO I ASK THAT YOU BE UNDERSTANDING ABOUT THAT.

ファウ ファウ ファウファウ
1998. INSIDE BERLIN, (FORMERLY EAST) GERMANY.
NOT CROSS THE POLICE LINE DONT RO
WEEOO WEEOO WEEOO WEEOO
MEIN GOTT... SUCH A VILE ACT...
VAT'S THE MATTER? VAT ON EARTH HAPPENED?
I HEARD THE CHURCH VAS ATTACKED!!
EXPLAIN THE SITUATION, ANDERSON.
!
MAXWELL, EH...BEEN AE LANG TIME.
SAE ISCARIOT IS FINALLY HERE...

◇BONUS STORY
クロス　フアイヤー
CROSS FIRE②

THE TARGET WAS OFFERED MONEY BOUND FOR THE VATICAN TOMORROW MAIRNING.
A' THE WINTER SEASON OFFERINGS FAE GERMANY'S EASTERN REGION WERE GATHERED HERE.
EIGHT PRIESTS AND NUNS WERE KILLED, FOUR BADLY INJURED, AND AE WHOLE $3,700,000 WAS TAKEN.
HMPH. THEY WERE CERTAINLY FLASHY ABOUT IT.
...SO WHAT WAS THEIR AIM?
AYE, TAKE AE LOOK AT THIS.
LOOKS LIKE THEY ARE NAE JEST YER USUAL OLD-FASHIONED ROBBERS.
SHF
SKFF
R'JEST YER USUAL OLD-FASHIONED TERRORISTS.
"TRUE LIBERATION TO ALL REVOLUTIONARIES WORLDWIDE!!"
...THE PRICE OF BLOOD IS A HIGH ONE.
THESE ANTI-CHRIST COMMUNISTS WILL PAY WITH THEIR SOULS!

White Dolphin
RED LION
WANT TO GET A DRINK?
NEIN, DANKE.
VE'RE ALMOST THERE.
THIS IS SUCH A DRAG, THOUGH.
CAN'T BE HELPED. IT'S FOR THE VATICAN'S SAKE.
I GOTTA WONDER. WHY IS THERE ALWAYS SOMEONE ELSE AGAINST US?
WE DON'T EVEN USE FORCE TO GET PEOPLE TO BELIEVE, THE WAY WE USED TO.
NO MATTER WHERE YOU LOOK, YOU WON'T FIND ANOTHER RELIGION OVER-FLOWING WITH SO MUCH LOVE, GLORIOUS AND PERFECT.
SO WHAT'S THE DEAL?

THERE'S ZIS PROBLEM THAT HAS NEVER QUITE DIED OUT.
BELIEFS COME IN WARIOUS FORMS.
VRRRRN
GCHAK
GCHAK
I WONDER IF THERE ARE ANY BUDDHISTS LIKE US TWO?
I REALLY HAF NO IDEA.
VELL, GUESS THIS IS IT.
STAYING IN A HOTEL WITH MONEY YOU STOLE FROM SOMEONE...
...PISSES ME OFF!

50 NORINCO 86S BREECH-LOADING RIFLES.
200 TOKAREV T-33 AUTOMATIC PISTOLS.
120 AK-47 ASSAULT RIFLES.
150 KILOGRAMS OF C4 PLASTIC EXPLOSIVE. 300 ELECTRICAL FUSES.
ALL TOLD, $2,572,760.45.
...DO YOU INTEND TO START A WAR OR SOME-THING?
ARE YOU ***SELLING*** OR ***NOT?***
I THINK I WILL!!
WE'LL ***SELL*** TO ANYONE WHO HAS ***THE MONEY.***

OKAY!!
WE HAVE A DEAL.
I DON'T KNOW WHO YOU LOT REALLY ARE.
AND I DON'T KNOW ANY DETAILS.
STAND
THE GOODS ARE ALREADY ON THEIR WAY.
す
INSPECT THEM, THEN TRANSFER THE MONEY TO ME TOMORROW.
BY THE WAY, I HEARD A CATHOLIC CHURCH IN BERLIN WAS ATTACKED...
AND A LARGE SUM OF DONATIONS WAS STOLEN...
WEREN'T YOU SUPPOSED TO NOT KNOW ANY DETAILS?
...AH, YES INDEED!
MONEY AND CLIENTELE ARE MY GODS, AFTER ALL.
GOOD DAY TO YOU.

BTAM
KATZ KATZ KATZ KATZ
PING
KATZ KATZ KATZ KATZ KATZ
KATZ KATZ KATZ
ROOM 903.
SIX MEN WITH HANDGUNS, ONE WOMAN.
SHE'S THE BOSS. AND... A KNIFE USER.
DANKE.

SO MANY FIRES TO DEAL WITH, EAST AND WEST.
THINGS ARE SHORTHANDED AND ULTRA-TIGHT. WE'RE ALWAYS RUSHING AROUND.
THEY DON'T PUT THEM-SELVES OUT IF WE STOP BURNING.
I ONLY WISH WE COULD BE AS BUSY AS YOU ARE.
VATICAN AMAZES ME, THOUGH.
TO THINK THAT THEY'D SEND GIRLS LIKE YOU...
AND SO, THE RIDGEWAY COMPANY OFFERS YOU ITS GRATITUDE FOR EMPLOYING OUR SERVICES.
WE OFFER DEALS IN ARMS, AMMUNITION, INTELLIGENCE, ETC.,
PREFERABLY TO THE HIGHEST BIDDER.
ズム
ZMMMM
WE'LL BE WAITING FOR YOUR NEXT JOB.
ズウ
ZMMMMN
LET'S GET TO IT.
PING

ILYU-SHIN.
CAN WE TRUST HIM?
FOOO
AS LONG AS WE'RE PAYING HIM.
WHAT CAN THOSE *HUMANITARIANS* AT THE VATICAN DO ANYWAY?
...BUT I HEAR THAT THE VATICAN HAS SOME ANTI-CHRIST COUNTER-TERRORIST SQUAD.
AND THERE WAS THE BEKA'A PLATEAU INCIDENT.
クイッ
FWP
YOU REFER TO THE ISLAMIC TERRORISTS WHO WERE WIPED OUT...
...BY THE TWO IN THE PRIEST AND NUN GETUP WHILE TRYING TO TAKE HOSTAGES AT THE RELIEF CENTER?
KNOCK KNOCK KNOCK
?!
!!

WHO'S THERE?!
TMP
UH, UM, A DELIVERY HAS ARRIVED FOR YOU...
A MR. RIDGEWAY LEFT SOME LARGE PARCELS FOR YOU AT THE FRONT DESK...
PEEK
LOOKS LIKE A DOOR GIRL HAS SOMETHING FOR US.
THAT SURE WAS FAST.
GCHAK
FOOL!! DON'T OPEN IT!

tink
SHLLP
ズル
SHIMA-BARA BATTOU IAI.
SHIN-DEN.
CHIK
BKAM
ドカ

CH!
CH-CHTO!?
TOO SLOW.
KBLAM
KBLAM
KBLAM
BLAM
KBLAM
BABABLAM BLAM BLAM
GHA
AH
SHF
SHFA

4
3
2
SHF SHF
SHF
5
KBLAM
LUNGE
GRAB
!!
WHOO

!!
GCHANG
FWUMP
WHOO
KLANG
KA!
KAHA!
YOU'RE THE ONES FROM THE VATICAN?!
YOU!
!!
!!

CHINNNG
!!!
SHM
YOU...'RE...
THAT'S RIGHT!!

!!
CHK
SHAA
POW
6
DMP
CHCHAK
NO!! STAY YOUR HAND, HEINKEL!!
I KILL THIS ONE!!

YOU STILL CLING TO GOD AND RELIGION TODAY?! YOU PARASITIC CANCERS LIVE OFF THE WORLD'S NATIONS AND PEOPLES!!
AND YOU STILL BELIEVE IN CHRIST!
LUNATICS!!
EVEN TODAY YOU DON'T BELIEVE IN GOD?!
HEH! YOU STILL BELIEVE IN COMMUNISM!
PUTRID REVOLUTIONARY FANATICS!!
JANG

SHIMA-
BARA
BATTOU
IAI-
RYUU!!
TEN-
ZAN!!
CHAK
SHUT
UP!!
VWOO
CHINNNG
NGA?!
PING

BLOOSH
AH AAAAA
BTUMP
BTUMP
AHH!
NO AA
UO AHA
GUO AHA
AA AAA!
YANK

*note: Russian for "Bread for bread, blood for blood..."

BEEBOOBOOP BEEBOOBOOP BOOP BOOP
TI4
TI4
TI4
KCHK KCHK
KCHK
CLK RINNNG
RI-RINNNG RINNNG CLICK
AH, CHIEF. IT'S ME, HEINKEL.
GICHIK
IT'S OFER. THEY'RE ALL DEAD, JA. BUT...
...JA.
VAS THAT VAT YOU VANTED?
BDOOM!

THE FOLLOWING DAY, THE VATICAN.
A MASSACRE?! OUTRAGEOUS!
YES. THAT IS THE ORDER I GAVE.
SECTION XIII SHOULD BE A MORE AGGRES-SIVE GROUP.
WHEN SOMEONE WIELDS VIOLENCE AGAINST THE VATICAN...
...IT SHOULD BE PREPARED TO REACT, WIELDING EVEN GREATER VIOLENCE BACK.
TH-THAT'S ABSURD!
THEN WHAT OF THE VATICAN'S HUMANI-TARIAN IMAGE...?!

BUT ANTI-CHRISTS AND HEATHENS...
...ARE NOT EVEN HUMAN.
THEY ARE INSTRUMENTS OF SATAN, HINDERING THE KINGDOM OF GOD.
HE'S INSANE...CREEPY!
THESE THINGS MUST BE HANDLED QUIETLY, SO EVEN IF THEY MUST DIRTY THEIR HANDS...
...THAT IS WHY THOSE TWO, AND WE, WERE CREATED.
"FOR DOGMA WE WOULD KILL EVEN OUR FOUNDER."
IT IS THAT FANATICISM THAT IS THE FOUNDATION OF ISCARIOT, WHICH BEARS THE NAME OF JUDAS HIMSELF.
JESUS
WE ARE THE EARTHLY AGENTS OF THE VATICAN'S DIVINE PUNISHMENT.
IT IS WHAT SECTION XIII ISCARIOT WAS CREATED TO DO!!
CROSS FIRE / END

THE AFTERWORD
JAN'S
A MERRY MANGA
LUKE'S AND
LIFE'S A PAPER BALLOON
BEAUTIFUL PEOPLE CORNER
ビューティホーのピーポー
HI THERE! MY NAME'S JAN! HOW ARE YOU DOIN'?! I'M REAL HAPPY I WAS ABLE TO MEET ALL YOU FOLKS! HOPE WE HAVE A GOOD TIME TOGETHER!!
BY THE WAY, I GOT BURNED TO A CRISP.
I GOT EATEN.
BY A DOGGY.
WHY'VE I GOTTA GO THROUGH
SUCH A PAINFUL THIIIIING?
ボエーーー
AWOOOOOO!
I GOT EATEN BY A DOGGY.
WITHER IN THE DAYTIME, GOOD AS GONE BY NIIIIGHT.
FINISH WHAT I GOTTA DO, ROLLIN' ROUND AND ROUND.
ゴロゴロゴロゴロゴロゴロゴロゴロ
ROLL ROLL ROLL ROLL ROLL ROLL ROLL ROLL
BY A DOGGY...
完
THE END

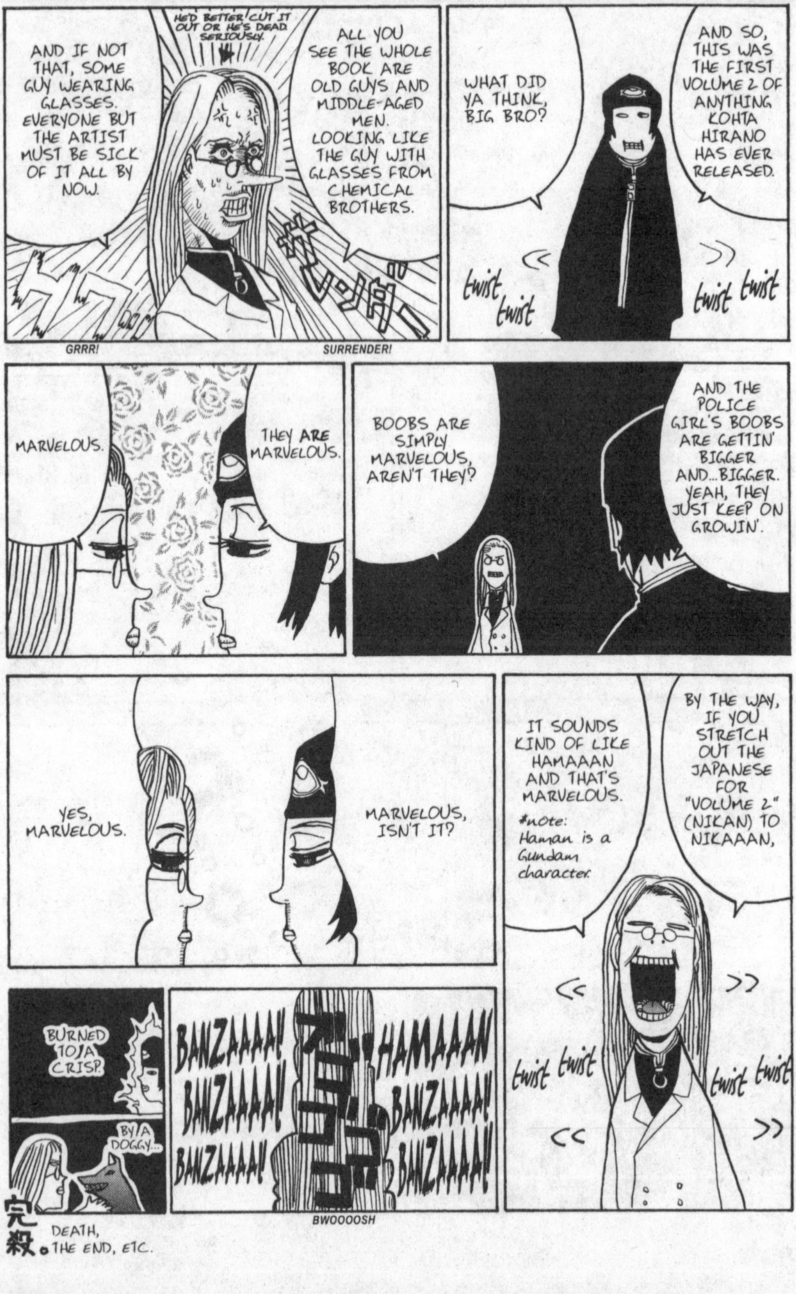
AND SO, THIS WAS THE FIRST VOLUME 2 OF ANYTHING KOHTA HIRANO HAS EVER RELEASED.
WHAT DID YA THINK, BIG BRO?
twist twist twist twist
ALL YOU SEE THE WHOLE BOOK ARE OLD GUYS AND MIDDLE-AGED MEN. LOOKING LIKE THE GUY WITH GLASSES FROM CHEMICAL BROTHERS.
HE'D BETTER CUT IT OUT OR HE'S DEAD. SERIOUSLY.
AND IF NOT THAT, SOME GUY WEARING GLASSES. EVERYONE BUT THE ARTIST MUST BE SICK OF IT ALL BY NOW.
SURRENDER!
GRRR!
AND THE POLICE GIRL'S BOOBS ARE GETTIN' BIGGER AND...BIGGER. YEAH, THEY JUST KEEP ON GROWIN'.
BOOBS ARE SIMPLY MARVELOUS, AREN'T THEY?
THEY ARE MARVELOUS.
MARVELOUS.
BY THE WAY, IF YOU STRETCH OUT THE JAPANESE FOR "VOLUME 2" (NIKAN) TO NIKAAAN,
IT SOUNDS KIND OF LIKE HAMAAAN AND THAT'S MARVELOUS.
*note: Haman is a Gundam character.
twist twist twist twist
MARVELOUS, ISN'T IT?
YES, MARVELOUS.
HAMAAAN BANZAAA! BANZAAA!
BANZAAA! BANZAAA! BANZAAA!
BWOOOOSH
BURNED TO A CRISP.
BY A DOGGY...
完殺。 DEATH, THE END, ETC.

*note: The Zakrello was one of the first models of mobile armor developed in *Mobile Suit Gundam*.

HAILING FROM ADACHI WARD, TOKYO

HOBBY = HARASSMENT, CHINKO IJIRI, BEING ANNOYING, BEATING OFF.

FAVORITE SPACE FORTRESS = A BAOA QU.
*note: This is another *Gundam* reference.

OBNOXIOUS FAVORITE OJAMAJO? = HAZUKI.
*note: This refers to the anime *Ojamajo Doremi*.

FAVORITE WRESTLER? = HANAYAMA. GRAPPLER.
*note: Once again an anime reference. This time it's to *Grappler Baki*.

FAVORITE NEWTYPE? = HAMAN KARN.
*note: Yet another *Gundam* reference.

WHAT DO YOU WANT TO BE IN YOUR NEXT INCARNATION? = MAHARAJA KARN, THEN GIVE BIRTH TO HAMAN.
*note: I don't think I even need to explain at this point.